Blacc Luv

A fictional novel written by Celestinia Bishop

06/2019

Chapter 1.

The eerie appearance of this room, the squeaks from the stage, the spine shivering music that echoes the auditorium, hearing the voices of people I never met, seeing the eyes of people as they hunch each other trying to figure out who I am, the sniffles of noses and the cracking of recycled tissue paper.

I stand before this crowd of unknowns, and I began to speak: As a little girl you always question the stories you read about in fairy tales, wondering if the myths of finding a knight with shining armor holds truth. Well in the real world of life and lessons.

"I found my "Knight" but that was a mere description of his skin complexion and his "Armor" was a metaphor used to describe his package"

I recall the day I met the best thing that ever happen to my heart like it was yesterday. Renae and I became friends a few months prior, instant best friends, because both our dudes were incarcerated in Wayside Pitchess Detention Center on different criminal complaints, they shared the same dorm, so they have daily contact with each other.

Therefore, when Malik couldn't make a call collect to me, his homeboy Bassboy would on his behalf and have his girlfriend Renae to contact me and vice versa. As these two community rejects hustle me and Renae out of our time and energy while doing their bids, Renae and I became very close acquaintances.

Although mentally I was more mature than Renae not because of social development, but because of hardship. Although we both were the same age, our lives were very much different than alike, but we had more common ground than negative reflection.

Renae's parents were both alive; shared co-parenting and remained friends after their breakup, unlike me, she had a cosby show family togetherness.

As a teenage single mother of a soon to be one-year old daughter, I fought extremely hard for my graduation's credits. I knew I had the odds stacked against me when I became impregnated by an adult man, who didn't even take the time out to see if I ever had the kid or not. I finally graduated at the age of sixteen from Crenshaw Continuation in Los Angeles, California.

When Renae and I met she was in her last year of high school, with no kids, and had several acceptances to colleges with a bright future ahead of her.

Our friendship was completely different than ones I had before. Mainly all my prior friends were gang bangers, drug dealers, uneducated junior high school dropouts, looking for a purpose in life, from examples not fit to lead a horse to water.

Other associates I had acknowledged their self-worth for what it was and where it wasn't going. But not all my friends were misfits, just lost looking for a possibility to become great at something special.

Therefore, each relationship was dealt with according to the relevance it played in my life at that time.

Now Renae's friends were weird at least too me, she had a strange way of embracing her friendships. Some of her friends could never be on my level mentally, I was already a grown woman trap in a child's body.

I was already living the life of a grown ass women. Being a single parent, experiencing responsibility firsthand, having to pay bills on a budget, sacrificing myself for another, things they could never imagine at this young age.

I'm sure that majority of Renae's friends frowned upon me for being so young with a child. But I didn't care, there youthful opinion of me never paid a bill or brought any diapers, so it was like wind beneath my wings. Renae's friends she introduced me to appeared to be more focus on social escalation versus real life dilemmas. I used to call them "Clueless Bimbos".

Then it was the "Undercover Hoes" pretending they weren't like that but were the main ones ready to suck a nigga dry in a dark closet at her best friend's Mama's house.

I noticed the messy ones also; you know the ones that started shit then forgot how shit got started. Last but least was her friend named Nikki, couldn't quite get her come off, she appeared to be a liar, and very sneaky, always trying to act safe, or passed off as being naïve and unaware. Nevertheless, that was Renae's friend so I compromised some, but I really couldn't stand that little Bitch.

One day in mid-November 1991, Renae called and asked if she could borrow my blow dryer, I told her yes then ask her how she was going to get it? Renae stay several blocks from my house, and I was not going to meet her halfway this time, because I just put my baby to sleep.

Renae said she had a ride and would be there shortly to get it. Renae came, I buzzed her in our apartment complex, and we chatted a bit in my living room, but she had to hurry back outside because her ride was out front waiting.

I walked Renae outside and sitting in the awaiting Nissan Sentra was a sexy ass looking young nigga. Not sexy because he was fine as fuck, but the sexy in chocolate skin completion, thug, rough, I been to the county jail type. That young gangster sexy, that confident and secure sexy, the kind that knew his dick was extra big for his sagging khakis sexy, the I will fuck you dry and have you putting your panties on backwards type of sexy, the I will definitely have you walking with a gap sexy. This dude was just my type.

Before Renae got on the passenger side of the car she turned and look at me, and smiled, the type of smile where her eyes were saying *"Bitch he fine huh"*?

When Renae got in the car, she introduced Blacc to me. *"Blacc that Stacy my gangster friend with the kid I was telling you guys about the other day".* Blacc replied *"What's Sup"* with a quick head nod. I think I paused for a second or two and responded with a *"Sup"* and a slow licking of my lips, like boy you already know what's up or what could be.

I noticed see Blacc eyes as he looked up towards me, that he knew what my "Sup" meant.

I never met someone that I knew right off I wanted to fuck the shit out of before today. It was crazy how I became instantly infatuated by this young ass nigga, and we only said hello to each other.

I have met niggas before, but never ever did bells and sirens go off in my head. I never was discombobulated by anyone's presence. This shit was weird as hell. I hurried to wrap this conversation up, because I felt out of character. I needed a distraction so I could regain my composure. "Alright girl I said, call me later" as I slowly walk back towards my apartment building, deep inside I hope he wasn't watching me walk away.

Later that week, Renae was in Bellflower, California at Blacc's house. Renae called me from his number and told me that her and Nikki were chilling over there. Renae explain that Nikki and Blacc was in a relationship.

I was unbothered by that information, but it made me want to fuck her man Blacc even more so now, all because I didn't like Nikki.

As me and Renea talk, and laugh on the phone, I would slide in general comments and questions about Blacc, not too obvious but more informational.

Renae and I talked and laugh about nothing important for hours as we always did daily, but somehow one of us ended the call with a "*I will call you back*". When I returned the call, Renae had already left to go back to Hawthorne where we both stayed.

I called the unlisted number from my caller ID box. Blacc answered and told me she had left already, so I hung up.

Few days later Blacc's number was again on my caller ID. I didn't immediately call back; I waited a few hours until I knew for sure that Renae and Nikki were back in Hawthorne then I called his phone. Blacc answered, *"Hay Blacc this Stacy is Renae still over there she called me some time ago and I'm returning her call?"* Blacc replied *"Naw they left"* I took that as no her and Nikki both not there. Good for me I thought as I'm listened to his voice melt in my eardrums like cotton candy in my mouth.

Blacc's voice was deep and inviting so I started an innocent conversation that lead to us to talking a few hours that night, Blacc ended the call with, *"I will call you tomorrow, I got to get up for work in the morning"*.

I didn't really think Blacc would call the next day, and he didn't, but he did the day after, and each time we spoke, I grew more and more mentally involved with him. Our small talks became full blown conversations, and never once did he openly express that Nikki was his girlfriend nor was, he unhappy.

Matter of fact his conversations were just the opposite, like when will I see you, and the times I needed to call him. Over the course of almost two months I felt I knew him. I felt we somehow connected.

I could tell that an attraction was forming between us; all those nightly conversations were leading me straight to his bedside.

The days before the approaching New Year, Blacc and I planned to spend it together. I was going to his house in Bellflower on New Year's Eve and spend the entire night with him. I was finally going to experience the physical sensation of him.

I rode the RTD all the way to his house. I left my daughter with my grandmother for the weekend. Once I got to the bus stop near his house I got off and he was waiting there waiting for me. I think he thought I wasn't coming, and I thought he was low-key trying to set me up. But curiosity killed the cat.

I needed to find out if this attraction was real. We walk back towards his apartment hand in hand, with me finally really looking him up and down, damn this little nigga is sexy as fuck. Shaved bald head, thick broad shoulders, medium muscles, strong spaced apart shoulders, he was country thick and solid, but his eyes were misleading, his lips were small but suckable, he was tall and climbable, overly handsome and he was chocolate, which was my favorite part of him. Blacc's skin tone was smooth and shiny, you could tell Blacc had many women by the way he walked and spoke.

Blacc was just too cocky to be a pretender.

Blacc's hospitality was cool for a bachelor's pad. I didn't expect too much, he had already disclosed to me that he worked for Pepsi and was roommates with one of his male cousins.

Overall their apartment was cool for some young ass nigga's spot. We all sat in the living room for a while, ate pizza and drank Pepsi, which he had plenty of, go figure. Then around ten o'clock the two of us went into his room, it was dark, I can't even recall if he had a light in there at all.

I remember getting comfortable, taking off my shoes, and laying across his bed, while I adored his movements in and out the bedroom. Then we both lied parallel to each other, Blacc scoped me closer to him, and gently kiss my lips, and with each peck became stronger than the last.

Blacc passionately inserted his tongue down my throat. rough and tender at the same time, so unbelievable. Blacc's kisses made me so wet, then he begins to bring me closer and closer, while his tongue is thrust down my windpipe.

Now his body was fully on top of mine. I felt his package getting harder and longer in his pants. The way Blacc laid on top of me was perfect. I could feel his manhood with every stroke, him pressing against my pussycat, grinding from side to side, he's making me even more moist.

I could feel the heat between my legs, my underwear becoming soaked by his erotic foreplay, never knew dry humping could cause such an eruption.

I never felt like this when we use to play hide go get it as a child.

Blacc is aggressively opening my legs, wider and wider, as he grinds harder and stronger. Blacc begins to undress me, forcefully but not impatiently. I lay there and wait till he finishes, I'm completely naked watching his silhouette undress, he slides his pants off then begins to remove his shirt in a teasing motion, before I could get into his striptease he lays right back on top of me.

Blacc's hands reach under my ass cheeks, holding tight, Blacc is teasing my pussy with his dick head as he's making it jump up and down. We start kissing again, this time more aggressive and intense, sucking each other's tongues and lips.

I'm now begging for him to enter my body. Once his dick head reached the opening of my vagina, I nut quick, hot, sticky, and super wet.

I look in his eyes and I could tell he enjoyed my welcome package. Blacc looks me straight in my eyes as he began to go deeper and with every stroke our bodies are becoming one.

I grip his dick with my inner walls, holding on tight and pleasurable. Blacc couldn't resist.

Blacc was a freak no doubt, but tonight I was ready for all the sexual encounters he wanted to share with me. We fucked damn near in any position you could think of. I rode him, doggy style, 69, 68, legs up, legs closed, spread apart, choking, fast, slow, standing up, bending over, sitting down, on the bed, off the bed, holding the wall, on the wall, against the wall.

Whatever he wanted, I wanted to give it to him. Hours and hours passed, we will break between his explosions and start right back where we left off at.

Blacc's endurance was that of a young fit football player in Pop-Warner. It was like we were two crazed animals fighting over who had more sexual control over the next.

I never been fucked and felt like this before, he broke my mental cherry, I had multiple orgasms.

Before today I thought I knew what an orgasm was, but I guess I didn't know shit. Blacc had my body shaking, jerking, bending and twisting in directions I never knew were remotely possible. Blacc's loving made me fuck him back, as his body took me on a mental ride; I think I fell in love. Every thrust of his dick going in and out I knew I was his, and he kept feeding me more and more.

I deserved every piece he had to offer.

At times our sessions were straight from a porn movie. "That white people shit". Throughout the night Blacc would pace his stroke, slowly feeding me his dick. Blacc made me want him, crave him, my body became his.

I was sexually ready for whatever he wanted to give or do. I felt like I had known him all my life. Blacc's room riddled with our aroma, his bed sheets wreaked of our passionate sexual explosions.

I remember laying on top of him after he made his final deposit, I could feel my body soaking up his seeds. Blacc became my habit. I was now addicted to him.

As I laid there wishing this would never end, how I dreamed of this before, I think I'm sprung. How could one person have so much sexual desire in their body to share with another person.

As the gunshots faded away, and fireworks slowly painted the sky, even when the echoes of the emergency vehicles racing back and forward ended, we laid there cuddled up.

Blacc holding me tightly on his chest, with one hand holding my booty and the other softly placed and perfectly positioned across my back, I thought *"This was the best sex I ever had"* if I *ever forget my past I hope to always remember New Year's Eve* 1991.

Chapter 2

Who Blacc Was

I stayed at Blacc's house a few more days than I had expected after the holidays. Blacc left me alone in his house while he was at work. I made sure he got what he needed when he got off, me.

Blacc made sure his girlfriend Nikki stayed away all while I was over, even when she called I would do little shit like suck his dick so he could hurry off the phone, at this time I knew she wasn't competition, well at least not sexually anyway. Nikki spot was being filled by a woman that had the same sexual desire as her man had, what a perfect combination of lust.

Even though I dreaded leaving Bellflower, I needed to get back to my daughter. Blacc dropped me off and before I got out his car, he made sure I had instructions on how to keep in contact with him, and per his words I was now his boo-thang, and my pussy belonged to him.

During the next few months, Blacc started developing financial problems, I don't recall if he quit or was fired from Pepsi, but he became unemployed and to make matters worse his ass went to jail twice far for traffic tickets.

I recall one time he was in the Old LA County jail downtown, I went to visit him, I remember him being happy to see my face, before the visited was over I flashed his my pussy, so he could have some motivation while he's in the shower. On every visit, I always made sure I left a wet forty for his books.

As always when he got out, he came straight to my house to get me and take me home with him.

Our relationship was never branded with a stamp of commitment, I just knew I had a place somewhere near in his heart, and he owned mines.

It was a few times Blacc needed money from me, so he could re-up, or whatever it was that he did to keep money in his pockets, and I would give it to him no questions asked, that was my man, why wouldn't I help him out? I didn't have a problem with it if my daughter had the things, she needed prior to my offering to Blacc, I was good, now my grandmother had a major issue because I wasn't paying her no rent or helping on the bills.

When Blacc wanted to see me, I mean fuck me he would call or page me. We had codes for the pager, so I knew about how much time I had before he pulled up. Nine times out of ten when I got a paged, I wasn't coming back home that night for sure.

Blacc and I were always together, to the point where Nikki was no longer an issue of mine, as much as I wanted to tell Renae all about me and Blacc I promised him I wouldn't, and I didn't.

Blacc and I never had any disagreement; he never yelled or cussed at me, like he did Nikki. Blacc was just aggressive while we made love. Again, I could never say that he was committed to me, but I will agree that I knew I loved him, not just because we were sexually attracted to each other but because no matter what I could always be honest with him about anything.

By my eighteenth birthday in November of 1992, I was several weeks pregnant with Blacc's child. I never said anything directly to him about this baby, but truth be told I was ashamed I was pregnant with another kid and was so young.

My grandmother eventually found out, but at that time I was barely seeing Blacc, so it never mattered and when we did see each other, he never said anything to me about my stomach size. I wasn't big or really showing much, other than having a fat face and my little titties were getting bigger a tad bit, I hid it well.

I didn't take any prenatal pills or follow up with any doctors; I just wanted it to go away. I was embarrassed that I allowed myself to become pregnant again and less than two years after my daughter. Everyone already had a misconception about me and the first kid. What would they be thinking now?

I think Blacc knew and that's why he started getting really distance with me. This baby was not what we needed.

Especially, what I needed. I resented the fact that I was going to be someone's mom again, I already made one mistake, with all the free protection around I feel stupid for the dick and allowed him to bust freely without caution. I blame me. I had choices, and I didn't use any of them, now I stuck in a situation that could have been prevented. I was already struggling trying to keep some stability for my Daughter, another mouth to feed, I practically starved myself, and I never wanted any more children.

As Blacc and I grew apart, our getaways became far too less, it seems he would only call or come by when he needed some money or sex.

I was beginning to feel used. Like I knew deep inside I wasn't the only person he was seeing at this time, it was someone else besides Nikki, his time was limited.

Depression began to consume me, I went back to hanging out with the homies, ripping and running the streets, Blacc was gone and I honestly felt this kid ran him off. I felt he knew and thought I was trying to trap him, only if he knew the truth, this baby was an honest mistake on both of our behalf.

Last time I saw him was in May of 1993, when Blacc called requesting some money from my county check. I delivered on June twenty first nineteen ninety-three.

A little Girl, full term, wavy hair, bright matte grey complexion, three pounds and dead. I was able to hold her lifeless body for a few minutes after birth. I whisper her name gentle in her tiny ears, "Shy"!
Because of my selfish immature ways, I killed her.

I was to shame to help this defensive soul, who depended on me to protect her from the awaiting world of evil I left the hospital with a sealed box of her remains paid for by my grandmother, who promised not to ever tell a soul.

Months later I was told that Blacc went off with Renae and Nikki to college somewhere in Mississippi. I hated life after that and vowed to be as broken hearted to any man I had going forward.

Sex was no longer meaningful to me, I loved Blacc and he still ended up leaving to fend for myself in this big world of savages.

Although I was again abandoned by love, I should have known my goods was only for the getting. As wicked and evil as it seems, I missed him more than I ever loved that baby.

Chapter 3

I gave it to God

Although I haven't seen nor heard from Blacc in almost a year, I often thought about him, sometimes I wonder how things would have been if my daughter survived.

Would he had returned knowing that he had a family?

Unfortunately, when I did have thoughts of those kind, I would also dread the day I would see his face. He betrayed my trust in us.

I shared my most intimate secrets with him. I open a lot about who I was and things I experienced growing up, things that could haunt and hurt me in the long run if he ever shared my secrets with a person who wanted to see me hurt. I lost my friend because I was in love with a loveless lover.

I know that Renae returned home from school because we hooked back up. Renae told me all kinds of stuff transpired when her, Nikki and Blacc when they went off to college.

How Nikki and Blacc used and betrayed her, then bounced with outstanding bills due and payable. I thought that was fucked up, how could Nikki treat her friend like that over a worthless nigga.

I'm sure there are always two sides to a story, but I kind of believe it when I was told he use to beat Nikki ass, she look like the type to let a nigga punch on her and suck him up with her busted lips. Blacc appeared to just have a habit of destroying good shit and loyal women.

I started back dating a few dudes here and there, but no-one was him or compared to him. I'm sure I missed out on a few decent guys because my heart belonged to a disappearing lover.

I eventually moved out of my grandmother's house to a single apartment in the Mid-Wilshire district. During this time in my life I became more focus on being a mother to my growing daughter and writing music for a few upcoming artists at Island Records.

On day I just happen to go by my Grandmother's house and while I was there Blacc pop up. A sight for sore eyes, but this time my heart didn't beat fast, I didn't pause, I don't even recall if my facial expression changed, all I kept thinking while he was talking at me was *"why is this nigga here"*. He asked if *"we could go outside and talk privately"*, and at first, I was like *"No!"* Then he kept on talking, so I went outside to leave, and he grabbed my arm as we walk out the back gate.

Now for the first time ever his grab was forceful and mean, more leading me in the direction he wanted me to go. Blacc loudly said *"Get in the car"*, my smart-ass reply *"Look fool I aint got no money and I'm not trying to Fuck you! Whatcha want?"* I snatched my arm back. *"Stacy"* Blacc said just get in the car, *"Nope"*! I replied, *"We can talk right here. Matter of fact go back in the house and go talk to my Grandmama."* I turned and started walking headed towards Broadway. Blacc swiftly grab me, picking me up, carrying me towards this old ass car, he basically threw me in the front seat and slammed the door.

Now I'm think I'm supposed to be afraid, right! But this car was old ass fuck, the floor on the passenger side was gone, so I started to chuckle, like I know his ass can't be trying to kidnap me in something that looks like it needs a jump in order to start. Is he serious?

Blacc got in on the driver's side, and placed a gun between us, I guess that was his way of letting me know he's packing, I still wasn't scared.

I saw many guns before, what he thought? I was a street Bitch, low-key knowing he was strapped was a turn on, he is showing his thuggery side, if I wasn't so piss at him, I'm might have let him fuck me in that piece of shit ass bucket.
.
Surprisingly the bucket started without a jump or running kick start. Blacc squirted off with me riding passenger, I don't know where this fool is going, he is dipping in and out of traffic, hitting side streets and alleys.

Blacc pulls over in this dark area and ask the question I never wanted him to *ask, "Where's my daughter",* that's when I became afraid. How did he know, who told him?

How do I tell him she's dead, without him using this gun on me, all these thoughts ran quickly in my head? So, I thought smart, if I tell this little nigga the truth, he might pull the trigger and if I lie, I might be able to walk away.

So you already know what I did, *"Blacc I had a baby in June, she such and such age now, her name is Shy, but she's at my house, I came over to my grandma house to pick up my mail see, as I'm reaching in my purse to show him some mail with my name on it. I don't think he bought my story so I added, I will bring her over tomorrow".* Blacc insisted we go to my house now, and I reassured him I would bring her by tomorrow he can meet her, Blacc gave me his new pager number and told me to call him soon as I get back on sixty second.

Then the old Blacc returned and he ask for some pussy, told him I was on my period then he ask for some head, needless to say, I suck him off in a dark alley and he drop me back off at my grandma's house.

It was a few weeks before I went back over to my grandmother's house. I didn't want to run into him nor face the fact that the baby died. My grandmother said he came passed a few times looking for me, but after a while he stop coming pass. I still didn't think it was safe to return over there.

Sometimes being responsible you must take a few steps back in order to jump forward, and in my case, I moved back to my grandmother's house.

I feared every day I was there, wondering when Blacc was going to walk thru her front door, gun in hand, looking for a child that's in a box that rested on my grandmother television set in the living room.

Not to mention, my grandmother is fucking getting on my last fucking nerves, she complains about everything, but talk shit when don't nobody come around her drunk ass, she's confusing, she wants company but don't want nobody around. It must be the beers that got her crazy as hell.

I continued to see other men, even went back to this dude I knew wasn't no good, just because I needed the affection of a male companion. It was somebody familiar, but he was horrible to look at, he was the type you only saw at his house, he was not public material, but his heart was pure and honest. Absolutely the worst mistake ever, but his head game was amazing.

Don't recall how or when I saw Blacc, but this time, my heart stopped, I became discombobulated, and excited to see him. So much had happened in my life since we hadn't talk, and I needed my friend. I needed those listening ears, I needed his warm arms of embrace, I needed to feel like someone cared about me, and I needed him.

No matter how much distance came between us, every time I was in his presences it felt like time stood still, and all the hateful emotions I carried, unhealthy hate disappeared when I look in his dark misleading eyes.

Blacc had a way of melting my insides and massaging my heart into accepting whatever he had to give, good or bad.

Blacc and I talked about Shy, that one last time and we never spoke of her again; I cleared my conscious with him and God on the same day.

Chapter 4

Here today gone tomorrow

Well after my confession to Blacc, things wasn't quite the same, I look at him differently, even though he was in my heart, I don't think I loved him the same, it was like being hit by a train learning to walk again, sometimes you have the energy to take a step and the other times you like fuck it, it is what it is.

Our lives were going in a different direction, apparently someone must have told him to grow up and in doing so we grew apart. Unknowingly at this time he already had another child with a woman other than Nikki, which explained a lot of his vanishing ways.

We would get together occasionally, but nothing serious or consistent. I already had mentally prepared myself for this bipolar relationship after the second year of his off and on.

Just to remain friends at this point in my life was good enough, when I didn't hear from him in a while, I would call the county jail to see if that's where he was, sometimes yes and sometimes no, I just always hope he wasn't deceased, and I never got to tell him how much he really meant to me.

Blacc would out of the blue, keep in touch but nothing serious; I learn many months ago to stop chasing a man that loves to wander.

In my heart I still have passion for him, but it wasn't the same kind of lustful desire. I cherish your friendship more than our sexual experiences. In my short lifetime, I had been fucking with other niggas and had gotten fuck over by other niggas so basically what I did from here on out wasn't new or adventurous. It was a sick pattern of I use you, then you use me.

Sometimes I wonder was I even capable of really loving a man, without me thinking I was being used for something. Yes, prior to Blacc I had a daughter, but that relationship was a one-night stand, two homies that got together and had sex, no I am calling you tomorrow's, or good night pages, never had any what's up in traffic. My daughter didn't even know who her father was, and her dad didn't even remember I told him I was pregnant.

Besides my childhood boyfriend Malik that stayed in and out of jail, Blacc was my first real somewhat consistent, visual, touching, realistic relationship with a man I ever had besides the child molesters who prayed on my innocence to help their sick desires of youthful pussy.

The niggas I had before and after Blacc was just practice, niggas getting me prepare for real life relationships with more men who meant me no good.

One day out the blue I got a page, I knew this number but didn't recall where, I called it back thinking it was some nigga I met, old boyfriend I had, but it was Blacc. *"You miss me"* the voice said after I said hello.

I know this voice, I replied, "Hay *You*" *You miss me?* "If "I didn't then I wouldn't have paged"* the caller responded. I'm holding the phone smiling like crazy, pussy getting hot as fire, I replied *"When you going come see me"* he replied *"Right Now, where you at"* damn damn damn I'm thinking, Shit he can't come over here. I live with this nigga at his mama's house." *Oh, I'm not at home right now"* I said in a very dry tone, and before I could lie about my whereabouts Blacc hung up in my face.

I called back and told cuz the *real "Look you know my grandmother be tripping she put me and my daughter out and we in Inglewood at Tyrone's mama house off of Elm and Inglewood Ave, I could meet you around the corner if you like"* Blacc knew I dealt with this dude name Tyrone just as much as I dealt with him, the only difference between these two niggas was I loved one and tolerated the other.

When Blacc got closer to where I was, he paged me, I knew that meant to start walking down the street. Blacc pulled up in a white escort, windows dark as a flat screen television, music so loud my heart was scared to beat, and Blacc looking just as sexy as the last time I saw him.

We drove around a bit, really with nowhere to go, somehow, we ended up at Playa Del Ray beach, and while the moonlight was glowing inside the front window of his car, we were passionately fucking in his backseat.

Damn I missed this feeling. The feeling of him inside me seems like every time I allowed him a piece of me, I got weak for this nigga. How did this two timing, vanishing, womanizer have so much control over me, I asked myself. I must have been dick whip or just plain stupid for this nigga.

The next day came and I got that page, out the door I went, this time we went to Tyrone's sister apartments, the garage area was always pitch black and with his tint nobody would see.

Now this is where I fucked up at. I got that page and immediately left Tyrone's house and this crazy nigga followed me, and saw that I jumped in the car with someone, so when I got back, that nigga slapped the fuck out of me, not because he knew who I was with, but because he didn't know who it was.

Tyrone suspected it to be a nigga I was with. I couldn't fight him back nor really say too much, I didn't have nowhere to really go, and I had just given his mama some rent money.

The next day I called my boy cousin Lil D, to come get me and my daughter because this lame ass nigga slapped me, when Lil D got to Inglewood Tyrone tried to lie and say that didn't happen and was begging me to stay.

I knew my cousin way on his way, so my shit was already pack, so while this nigga was hoping and pleading with my cousin, praying my cousin don't beat his ass. I was putting our shit in his trunk.

When I got to my cousin house, he offered me the bedroom. I told him I was cool and took the living room. About a week or so passed and I invite Blacc over, who thought I was living with a nigga.

These guys are killing me they don't really want you, but don't want anybody else to have you neither. Blacc was on some you trying to set me up shit, but that wasn't the case, I really was on some hit this pussy type of shit.

Once Blacc met my cousin and saw that we were in fact cousins, he came over regularly. Again, this was a hit and miss mission of Blacc, he was so in and out my life, like he knew he could have me anytime he wanted.

I moved back into my Aunty house in Gardena, same place I first met Blacc at, then went back to my Grandmother's, I was unstable, from house to house. I lost contact with Blacc again.

Chapter 5

Imperial Highway

Now that I think my life was headed back on the right track, no more Blacc interruption. I started a relationship with this dude name Jason who lived in Compton.

Jason was friends of Renae, she introduced us a few years back. We kicked it before off and on, and yes, baby boy was packing big boy dick, he became my new Blacc.

I couldn't get enough of him, little taller than me, body was banging, light eyes, chocolate, waves, now this nigga was sexy as fuck, the complete package with dick game putting Blacc completely out my thought process.

Jason sexy was vivid, he was creative and pleasurable, he

enjoyed watching my body feed off his, he like for me to moan and wiggle, small outburst of *"Fuck me harder"* aroused his manhood.

Jason like to caress my body, rub and nibble, soft peaks of kisses on my lower back, and his wet tongue gliding up the center back crease as he rotate his tongue in a full circle on my neck opening his mouth to bite and suck on my neck, he love leaving passion marks behind on my high yellow skin, so the world would know he was there and what we did.

I adored the way he ate me out, his tongue sliding up and down on my click, how he inserted his entire tongue in my vagina tickling my inner walls, how the tip of his tongue peck and thump my click, he loved it when I came in his mouth, that's when he would go crazy, licking, sucking and slurping, it was like his mouth was a hoover vacuum cleaner.

 Jason sure knew how to please me.

Jason package was the longest, biggest I had so far, and he was my age, we weren't even twenty-one yet. I swear if I didn't know that it was real, I would have assumed he had implants. For him to be so young he was well experienced in the bedroom. I like the way he got us ready to enter mingle, he believed in foreplay and longevity sex. Jason could have been a porn star.

Although Jason lived in Compton, I always made a way over to see him at least three to four times a week. I craved his attention, when we were together, I felt safe.

Not safe as in protected, but safe as in nurtured and bonded. I think that's why I didn't really miss Blacc anymore, because the security I had in Blacc I found in Jason. Jason was trying to build me up verse Blacc method of tearing me down, same infatuation, but different love. Remarkable something that was new and different.

On the way to his house one day, my little bucket of a car had broken down. So, my cousin boyfriend James came over to take me to Jason house for a small monetary fee.

I telling my cousin boyfriend James how to get to Jason house, and we were talking and listening to the local radio station KDay and who did I see in the lane next to James car? Blacc!

Blacc look me straight in my eyes, recognized who I was, and didn't make any effort to say shit to me. I never in my life felt so low, my heart sunk in my chest, and I was fighting back my tears, how could he not acknowledge me? All the love I kept in my heart went right out the window; he made me feel like shit.

As I look back in the rearview mirror, I see him pulling up to a Bitch at the bus stop, getting at her. What did I ever do to him, to make him forget who and what I was to him? My soul wasn't ready for that type of rejection, all my happy disappeared.

That day set the tone for me to dog other niggas out. Someone mislead me, and my day of misleading was soon to come.

When I got to Jason house it wasn't the same, I really wasn't even excited to be around him anymore, in my mind I felt that if I allowed him in, he was capable of enduring that same hurt on me one day.

I was not mentally ready for this devastation. It was worse than the day I found out that Santa Claus was fake, and my grandmother really bought all my shit. All while I was physically in Jason presence, I still felt I left me on imperial highway.

Chapter 6

3636

It's been a few years since Blacc broke my heart on imperial Highway, after that day my whole dating agenda change.

My new motto was *"I'm loving them, when they are loving me"*.

Instead of feeling sorry for myself, I reinvented who Stacy was; I changed my nickname to the *"Westside Mama's"*. My new attitude was fuck over every nigga I meet and treat them like shit. I would never chase another man, he had to chase me.

I'm nineteen almost twenty, and I'm still not of a legal age to drink without ticketing. I change my appearance, that boy girl look was not becoming anymore. With age my weight picks up, not too much but it took me out the children section.

My mouth got slicker and more reckless, as an adult you feel honor to be able to verbally attack others without fears of getting slapped in the mouth by an elder. I was no longer passive in my male relationships; every action had some type of reaction, good or bad. It wasn't no longer okay to walk in my life and destroy me from the inside out. My voice was finally going to be heard and understood.

I was only physically attractive to dudes that dealt dope or had potential to end up in somebody federal prison one day, no more basic thugs. If a nigga wasn't pocketing or pushing, I didn't talk to them, not acting like I was better than the street hustler type, but I knew better than to subject myself to someone who's ability on lasted on a corner in the middle of a populated community, those types became more of a liability verse a come up.

I wasn't never afraid to ask a man, what his motives with me were firsthand, or explain to him what I expected from the start. Fair exchange wasn't no robbery.

I enjoy guys who like spending their money on me, I prefer to keep it this way, so I didn't feel used. Sexual contact was no longer, an important factor in my happiness, greed and self-gratification was. I could fuck myself at any given time; I felt I was giving honors if I shared me with someone else.

Majority of the time I didn't even have to fuck. Reckless experiences with men taught me conversations that became enough to mislead an individual into believing the words that graced upon my tongue.

Every man wants a woman who will openly share their body with them, so sex, now became just sex, a private interaction between two consenting adults, but it took a special kind of fella to want me to make love to and with.

Maybe my way of thinking and processing this strange adapting behavior had something to do with all the years I was molested as a child, having to replay all the times my body was manipulated by an unwanted person, as bizarre as it sounds my body became a weapon I used for protecting verses the many years I allowed it to be preyed upon, a force within a force, pussy power.

Secretly knowing that whoever I was with, didn't play me out of shit, but my time, and sometimes that cost a pretty penny, depending on the size and what he wanted me to perform.

Truth be told, I could have had a different dude damn near for each day of the week, it was something about my get down that attracted all sort men, thugs, or gangsters. Some say I had a flirtatious smile, a slighted grin that would melt hearts, I never saw that in me.

I always thought I mean mug everyone I met; perhaps they interpreted a twisted frown for a smiling face.

I mean it was a few times I had guys thinking I was really feeling them and set they ass up to get gank. Nowadays it was about survival. I didn't always have a ruthless and savage intent.

Only to the nasty perverts that wanted to use me, I just turned the tables around. I hung in places that I knew guys that like cute, sassy, sexy and flirty women.

Sometimes a quick come up was my motive, I had bills just like the next person, and a daughter to fed, what made my struggle any less that the next persons?

Not trying to pretend that because Blacc left I turned into this street bitch, no I was her before him, just so happening things work back in my favor. Although I was trying new ways to let out my life disappointments with Blacc verse making others my victim, but after he shifted on me in traffic, and since I could never get back what I gave him, I decided no-one will ever take me from me again.

I felt I didn't need that type of lifestyle with Blacc, but after him, I quickly converted back to my old ways. Just this go around instead of robbing drunk Mexican men for the money in their pockets, I began robbing nigga's that had a hidden agenda.

I don't know if my self-esteem was at an all-time high or my personal insecurities were at an all-time low. I thought I was the shit, and nobody couldn't tell me shit, the sun raised every day because I woke up.

I knew everything, especially when I started drinking, and smoking weed, my mind was floating and my body was numb, everyone became invisible to the outside world, if you weren't in my world you didn't matter.

My tools for self-control were disguised with self-destruction, until I got rape by one of my supposed to be homeboys. I knew what and when he did it, I just didn't recall how he did it, or why. Funny how drugs can intercept your mind into believing your untouchable until reality sets in and you get touch.

I was a victim again, but who would believe he did it. I had a lifestyle now that exhibits reckless and loose behaviors. I'm sure it will be someone chanting I deserve it, or I asked for it, only if they knew that my behaviors didn't invite a predator to violate me, he was sick and mentally incapable of having a natural sexual experience with a woman. Therefore, his only alternative was force and trickery. I didn't deserve it; it was an unwanted treason.

Night club hopping and sometimes erotic dancing at the stripper hangouts like club music staff on Florence Ave in Los Angeles. I was at the prime of my life, young, single, cute, and carefree and still not giving a fuck.

I had two or three solid dudes that took me on weekend

getaways every now and again, few boats ride down in the marina, couple of Atlantic City trips, fast cars and expensive hotel stays. This was not the life; I'm pretending on someone else's finances.

Dudes that made power plays that wore tailored suits, smoke cigars, went to board meeting, and had black cards, all had a different thinking process, it was like they were trying to build a women, it came with a lot of control mechanisms, I wasn't for sale, I really enjoy who I was and change only brought on rebellion. It was too late in my life for a father figure.

I like the guys who I could get money with, the illegal way, no more street hustling, standing on the corner serving bums, team sending out of state, and weeping the benefits of our product deliveries. I always been a loyal companion, if they were about that life so was I. With all the things I was doing, I never once thought about Blacc it was like that was someone who fell off the earth, he mentally died in my soul, and never in my wildest dreams did I ever think I would see him again. I no longer missed him.

Me and Jason hung out sometimes when I felt the need to get fucked by someone who gave a fuck about me, besides his good and super long piece always had a place in my wet pussy. Jason ate my pussy almost as good as Blacc did, and each time we fuck it always felt like the first time I had sex. Jason dick was so wide his forever strength the pussy to fit in; we need lube to just enter my body.

Although our physical attraction was bananas, I couldn't make him my only man, he had too many of Blacc's tendencies. Not by far did he disappear, mislead, vanish or have other women, he just scared me because he appeared to care, and I felt once I open that door, I gave him power, which would allow me to become victim to heartache. I cared deeply for Jason he was a stand up

Kind of guy, but I was living a life I knew he could adapt to, and he was too good to be ruin by my selfish desires of the world.

Chapter 7

Little girls don't make it with me

I was living in Inglewood in these apartments called 3636. that's where I befriended this heavy weight country chick name Steph at. Steph had a little girl and was carrying her second child. Steph and I developed a sisterly connection right off., she became my ride or die off top.

One hot Sunday evening Steph and I decided to walk to the store on Crenshaw Blvd which was about eight blocks away from our building, and that's when I met Dre.

This nigga looks like a model, he was about 27 years old, tall, fit, waves and chocolate, the way I like, I swear I have a type.

Dre made my heart beat faster, me stutter, he had that Blacc effect on me, and I needed to regain my thinking.

I walk out the store he was walking in, and his body rub mines, I felt his gun on his side as he slightly brush me, I said, *"Don't hurt nobody with that"* Dre replied *"I won't intentional hurt nobody, it's for my protection!* "So immediately I said, "I *will protect that any day"*, he smiles and continued to walk in the store, looking back to see if I was still watching him, and I was. Before I got to the end of the corner Dre jump out of his car and handed me his number and said, *"Call me in an hour, let's go to dinner"*. I took that piece of paper and tucked it in my front pants pocket, praying I don't lose it on the way home. We had dinner that night, edible snacks you can't digest, yeah Dre was a whole appetizer and I was full off the introduction itself.

It was always something about them chocolate brown dudes that turned me on, and this nigga dick was bomb.

Dre had a different way of making love to me, it was special, he really nurtured my body, and it wasn't about wham bam with him. Dre fuck me mentally. His physical physic was hand carved by God, he was smooth with gangsterism, and his love making was rated x and inviting.

Dre taught me how to fuck him back from the bottom, how to take each stroke, breathe in slowly, how to allow him to help he ride him on top, with his hands under my thigh area, bringing me down on his dick. Dre was the first man to ever eat the booty, stick his tongue inside my ass hole, move it in and out, lick the rim of my butt, sucking and kissing it. When he first did it, that blew my mind, I was scared at first, but he instructed me to relax and it will be ok.

I swear it was a heavenly experience, I suggest everyone try it once, and that right there made me hooked on him alone. Dre instantly became my main dude, but I still had a few sides for some get money shit.

Dre wanted or perhaps thought I was his only one, but Blacc Fuck up my commitment to anyone. I never put the stamp on any relationship after Blacc. I just made myself available when Dre needed me to come sits on his face and ride his good dick.

This other dude name Luther I met right after Dre was young ass fuck, barely twenty-one, but balled the fuck out. OMG his body was massive, he lifted weights and shit.

Luther wasn't attractive, but his money made him fine as fuck to me, he could dress his little ugly ass off, his clothes help make him attractive.

Money everywhere, cars, jewels, houses and he was married to this older lady who was a real estate investor and she spoiled him rotten.

I used to fuck him at their house while his wife slept in the next room. I like the way he made me feel sexually, that sneaky shit was a turn on, I think I had a type, thick and chocolate, or was I trying to reinvent a pretend Blacc, long as the nigga show traits of Blacc I was feeling them heavy, it was always something I couldn't explain.

I used this nigga Luther for his money and dick. But eventually I started falling for all the materials things he offers in exchange for my loyalty. We made major money together. I connected him with dudes I fucked on or used to fuck with. Dealing with money everything you do is business; therefore, you learn not to take some deals personal.

I was really feeling this dude Luther, I didn't cut Dre loose, but I did put him on the back burner.

Jason was out the picture completely. No more sex visits or phone calls, I left him alone totally, when he started stress some only us exclusive shit, I aint gone even lie, I scared of commitment.

34

Because I was getting so emotional attached to Luther so tough, when I found out he had another me floating around, and not his wife. The shady Westside Mama quickly ended his relations with his wife, kids, and that other woman he had in them streets.

I don't need to explain what I did, all you need to know is that cuz was still breathing but got a little more muscular from his extended stay, all drug deals aint good ones.

While I stayed at 3636, I also befriended a lady by the name of Evette, she was gay, but had a daughter prior to her relationship with her lady friend Evonne.

Their apartment was right in front of mines, so we could just open the door and talk to one another if we wanted to without even leaving our residence. Yevette was strange she wore weird ass hair do's, spoke very loud and raspy, but cried a lot, something in her life was just as dysfunctional as mines. Maybe that's why we instantly connected, two lost souls looking for acceptance from somebody, wanting to feel useful in any way possible, I understood her misfortune.

Sometimes I was unaware if she sold drugs or use them, she had some erratic mood changes, but that could be a sign of mental illness, again something I was aware of personally seeing my grandmother switch reels in a second was unexplainable to others, something you had to see for yourself to believe. Evette act just like her.

Evette use to meet up with this dude named Kurt she uses to get work from. You could tell Kurt sold drugs, and I saying this based on the people that flocked his car when he drove up on Imperial highway. Like I said many times before if a guy had potential of someday ending up in a federal penitentiary, I was immediately attracted to him. I was addicted to that fast life, the life living on the edge, playing cops and robbers in real life. I know deep within I was missing something important in my life to attract those men in my life, but it was a mental rush, like a drug you can't shake.

One day Evette asked me to wait outside on imperial with her while she waited on Kurt to pull up, no problem I thought, I wasn't doing shit any ways. Kurt pulled up in a Camaro, Evette hop in the passenger side, they did they business, and when she got out, she introduced me to him, don't recall how we exchanged numbers but that's neither here or there, we hooked up that night on some we friendly fuck shit, two strangers sharing a moment, no promises of reaching out the next day , we just hooked up.

We both were sexually attractive to each other, like instantly. The chemistry was crazy, and his sex was amazing. He had this bed that was tall so he could beat the pussy standing up while I lay on my back.

Kurt was tall, his body was thick not fat but thick, his legs was strong, like he lift weights and shit, his body was semi carved, chocolate complexion, little lips, and his dick fit perfect wasn't overly big, but wasn't too little, nice round and ribbed. I enjoyed the way he beat the pussy up, he kissed were small pecks, like children kissing their parents on the cheeks. I could tell he was shy about some of the things we did, not that he was inexperienced just bashful kid like; it was kind of a turn on.

I would cum so hard on his dick it was crazy, I remember riding him till he filled me up with semen, the part about him that excited me the most was, Kurt could nut and his dick remained hard in his sleep, it was like a mental challenged to me, like little bitch you didn't shit I'm still up and ready, I never met a guy that could do that. Did I finally meet my match?

From the first night we slept together I was with him every night afterwards. I didn't care if he had a woman, he was with me at night all the time. I slept in his bed and that all that mattered he made me feel like I was special.

I low-key think Evette resented that she hooked us up, maybe her reasons were more of I hook you up and later he could hook her up with some more dope, she never thought we would be together in that way.

I was invested into him, one thing about Kurt he never exposed me to his work, our relationship was merely about us. I knew nothing about his street dealing besides what him and Evette did at 3636.

This was a pure relationship solely about us, the two of us, we would talk while he held me at night, I would investigate his face while he slept, feeling like I never wanted this to end.

I think I was falling for a nonaffiliated, a guy who lived recklessly without being reckless, I swear I have set dudes up before, but this was one dude I would have took a bullet for, did a jail bid for if I had to save him, he was perfect for me in ways that was unexplainable, but priceless. Each morning I left I always wanted to return in his awaiting arms for some reason.

Because now Evette's in her feeling about me and Kurt, she slowly started mentioning that he had a wife, a small kid, where he lived, other women he had, and what really made me think was when she told me her and him use to fuck often as a trade for drugs, that blew my mind.

I sleep with this dude every night and he is fucking bitches bareback for drugs. I don't ever want to die behind a sexual disease, that's my biggest fear in life, to suffer a slow painful death but the very thing I used to dictate my livelihood.

I didn't want to inhale half the things she was saying because I really thought him and I shared something beyond sex, but I knew he stayed somewhere else besides this back house he always took me to near Van Ness.

Kurt was the first nigga in the game, that I didn't care if he had money or not. I honestly adored him for him; if he would have gone broke, I would have remained around. His money never excited me he did, his presence in my life did.

I just can't keep putting my heart and body in places of danger. As much as I wanted to stay, I needed to walk away. I think it was in the best interest of doing so, I was emotionally attached, and he would have shattered my world with any kind of rejection from him.

Kurt never understood how much I loved him. I would have changed all my ways for him, he gave me something no one ever did, he took the time to find out who I was inside, he made me believe I was special to someone, he gave me hopes that my tomorrows will be us forever.

I was broken hearted, but he betrayed my trust, at any point in our situation he could have told me the truth about his dealing with these other women, I'm sure I would have understood my place in his life, and not to say I would have left, but at least I would have known what my options were beforehand.

I just stop calling him or returning his calls, it was a bittersweet acceptance on loving a man who adore many woman because his money gave him the rights to not hold regards to anyone's else feeling, his money didn't make him happy, it made him feel invincible, like he could buy everything and everybody, his pride wouldn't allow his to see that his ways are hurtful and misleading, but nevertheless I still loved him like I have never loved anyone else before him, damn Kurt why did you have to be so rap in the fast life when I was only trying to bring your life.

A few weeks went passed and I found out I was eleven weeks pregnant. I tried calling his pager number and he never answered, I think he was upset I just vanished on him, without an explanation, I get it, but dude please call back.

I reached out to Evette who still stayed in 3636 after I moved away, after bouncing on Kurt. I knew that she would have his contact information, they did business together. The update on Kurt that I got from her was he was in jail facing life, for drug trafficking. Here I am again in a situation I could have controlled but my heart was thinking when we were making love, my pussy was.

I wasn't going to put my body in any more unexplainable situations, besides why would I keep his child knowing it will never meet its father.

Although I thought about keeping the baby because he gave me something special, and maybe his gift was to teach me how to love another the way he loved me back, I don't know. I thought hard, like I could have been his peace, his fast life and Evette words took my man away.

I'm sure that I would have stayed down for him until the end of the world, but he never once ever gave me the impression he cared for me just as much as I cared for him.

What was my world really coming to? Mental and physical abuse caused because I cared for men who cared less about me? I had an abortion before I reached five months, seems like little girls don't make it with me.

Dre never knew about any other person I was with, when I wasn't with him. Therefore, me running back to his awaiting arms appeared to be more of a breakup let's get back together move.

I really did like Dre; he was my go-to when all else failed. If I was to ever get serious or settle down, he would have been my perfect life partner since Kurt was gone forever.

Chapter 8

Hello Stranger

My last two years was a trip, a journey to nowhere. I practically forgot who I was. I was stuck in a world of "Only Me". I didn't have time for my daughter, always had someone watching her. It was Me Me Me... Damn I lost control trying to be somebody I wasn't supposed to be, that wasn't who I was, no reality of how my life should have been.

I prove everyone who ever doubted me to be truthful in their opinions they had of me. I exhibited recklessly living, instability and irresponsibility to my parenting. Who did these streets create?

So I when I went back to being what I thought was normal, or as close to it as possible given my dysfunctional upbringing, and decided to let all that lust is not love go cold turkey, I lived off the coins I accumulated from deals and tricks and started to take life for what it was priceless.

I went back to college got my associates degree in business management, and now that I'm focus on living right. I would talk to Dre on and off. Even after he asked me to marry him, I just told him I wanted to wait till I was twenty-five at least for a commitment. He said he would wait.

I had a full-time job working at Fox Hills Mall as a cashier in my cousin Troy record store. My daughter and I had our own home, and I was single and celebrate. I even started attending church services regularly.

I had males' friends I would talk to occasionally, on the phone to pass the time away, but no-one at this time was making any personal house calls.

I would be to exhaust when I got home to do anything but feed my daughter, bathe and bed. My body needed the rest after two and a half years of street life.

Eventually Dre and I started back dating and this time we were doing it right, dates and dinners, us getting to know each other and the needs of one another. Slow walk on the beach at four in the morning watching the sun come up over the raging waves, smelling the salt and seaweed simmer in the tainted ocean water, as we glide across the soak sand our feet melting, leaving imprints of us behind.

Could it be that Dre was the real knight, here's to revise me from my past and bring better days of love and loyalty.

My grandmother was getting sicker and need someone to help her maneuver with her daily activities of living. I know firsthand that her and me living under the same roof was conflict waiting to happen, so I suggest my older cousin Coy who at that time needed a place to stay could go live with her, it was a win situation for the two of them, they can keep each other company, drink beer together, and Coy could watch out just in case our grandmother needed assistance.

Now my cousin Coy was act, even though she was older than me, her maturity level was that of an eighteen-year-old child. I think she resented me because she always made references to me acting like I was better because I had my daughter, had a job, and had money, a car and my own place.

I tried to encourage her all the time, I was happy she was going to school to do hair; I really was excited she finally found something to occupy her time.

One day I went to visit them, me and my little cousin Kita stayed for a few hours. I took a nap on my grandmother couch. Took them to the grocery store, and play spades with my grandmother, the vibe was nice that day.

My Big cousin Coy kept running in and out the house, I thought she kept going outside to smoke her weed, because everyone knew I didn't have those type of things in my life since I got rape. So, I never trip. She came back in and was like cousin "*My boyfriend had a cousin you should talk to*". Me knowing her taste in men, I will pass, I politely said "*Girl we don't date the same type of dudes*". Therefore, I happily declined the hook up. Before I could finish my forfeiting of the unwanted invite, she hands me the phone.

42

"Hello". I say the stranger says *"Hello",* she already told them my name, so he's asking general questions, I'm acting very evasive in my answering, then all of the sudden the stranger ask out the blue, *"Where Christina was"?,* I tell her girl I don't know who this is, but they must know me, I'm thinking about all the dudes I have dated, scared, tick and so on, who is this unidentified caller, I hand her the phone back, shaking my head in reference to I don't want to talk to nobody on no phone I don't know and who know me.

About ten minutes pass and my grandmother's door knocks, my cousin answer it her new boyfriend walks in and after she introduced him to us, the door open again and Blacc walks I, my heart drop, I'm in stock, I'm scared, excited, and mad at the same time, my grandmother on the other end is happy her friend is back.

Damn is all I thought, every time I get my life back in order, he finds a way to discombobulate my situations and focus.

Chapter 9

"A soul mate is someone with whom you can be yourself but is not necessarily a perfect fit." Although Blacc may have been good to me in a variety of ways don't necessarily mean he was good for me".

Life has a funny way of displaying your faults at your peak of understanding what life, and love is.

Now as I look into the eyes of the man who changed my perception of what a pure relationship should be, the person I believe would be forever my friend, the man who's child I carried, the person I trusted the most with me, the man who broke my heart, tarnished my soul, walk on my feeling, and who carelessly abandoned my potential, time and time again, the reason why I had sleepless nights, the reminder of all the tears I shredded and yet I still see a man I loved with all my ability.

I had no ill feelings towards him; in fact, I was honestly happy to know he was still alive. We talk awhile outside privately, did some brief catching up, exchanged contact information and said our goodbyes.

I didn't read more into this meeting other than two old friends seeing each other again. We both are different people now, I'm not the same sex stuck little girl I was and listening to his conversation I could tell he had matured a quite deal also.

I didn't immediately take advantage of his number; I think my heart was not allowing me to become antagonized by something that didn't belong to me, his love.

Blacc appear to be in a relationship, he didn't say he was, but he had the occupied demeanor, he disclosed the children he had now, and wasn't surprised.

I only had one child still. Blacc asked if I was in a relationship, I recall saying something to the nature of the word's kind of, we trying to figure it out, he shook his head and said, *"Well I know that a no"*.

We talk to each other here and there and one night we connected sexual again, it was like opening Pandora's Box, every part of me I tried to conceal was revealed when I let him enter my body. I felt like this was what I been missing, and what I search for endlessly in the wrong men, if only he knew he didn't malicious lead me in my past directions, but his accounts lead me on journeys only God could get me out.

Most men don't realize the simplicity they bestow on a hurting heart, mere conversations opens room for mental connection, and if you add a sexual desire of stimulation without reasonable thinking one may believe that the two share a mutual connection of togetherness, when in fact one is just enjoying the others company, and the other might think you're headed in a relationship. My pot of gold at the end of the rainbow.

His love making was different, his stroke had change, his pace was steadier and more uninterrupted, and his sexual concentration was more focus on pleasing verse his pleasure. It's was a different experience.

But enjoyable, somehow awkward. More satisfying than ever before, I remember crying soft tears of joy; it was like my heart was hurting a good hurt, self-cleansing.

Blacc was starting something I wasn't mentally ready for, Us. Not a relationship but US me being emotionally attached to what if's and should have been and would haves.

Yes, I enjoyed the time he was vesting in me, but my guards were up for his departure. Besides my guilt for cheating on Dre my conscious was wearing low and unbearable on my nerves. I needed to decide who and what I wanted.

Glad I didn't have to decide just yet. I was taking a trip to Alabama to go visit my daughter, which gave me time to sort things out. Reevaluate the importance both men played in my life.

While I was out of town, I spoke to Blacc almost daily. I ended up buying a car in Alabama and Blacc was going to come drive me back to California. Our plan couldn't go into motion my grandmother became deathly sick. I needed to hurry back to California.

Once I got back in town, Blacc made sure I visited her every day, even the days she didn't know who I was. My grandmother was hospitalized for almost three months, and I was truly grateful to have my friend by my side.

I didn't read more into what we were doing besides friends with benefits, did I think he was my man, no, did I know if he had someone else, but I didn't care. My only concern was I know he was there when nobody else was and that's all that mattered at this point.

One night after work I had some male company come over, a few fellas we all were just sitting around laughing and joking. When Blacc decided to show up unannounced, he didn't care that I had company, as he just walk in my bedroom like my apartment was his, he called my name out from the room, when I went I'm there Blacc told me it was time for my company to leave, I thought it was cute how he acting like he pays my bills.

The look in his eyes, I knew he was serious, so instead of having a rumble in my home, I thought it was in the best interest of everyone to call it a night. Blacc gave me thirty minutes to have all my male company out my house, I knew he was serious because after he said those words, he walk straight out my front door and didn't look back.

Now the Blacc, I know wasn't no punk and far from being a bitch, his hood name was Eastwood so you know cuz wasn't right in the head at all. I told my cousin Kita to come in my room, as she walk in I closed the door behind her, I'm panicking and moving back and forward I say *"Girl we got to get them out my house"*, Blacc will be back in thirty minutes, if they still here all hell might break loose, I might end up getting put out.

I telling her, *"I bet you he went and got a gun"*, my little cousin was looking all scared, and she replied *"Bitch they got to go"* I went back in the kitchen where everyone was sitting drinking and I told them I was super sleepy and had to get up early in the morning for work, the dude I was talking to said *"Stacy cuz you said you was off tomorrow"*, I said *swiftly "Look that's really my boyfriend and he tripping y'all got to go"*.

Long story short when Blacc got back everybody was gone, even my little cousin. Low-key Blacc turned me on being all aggressive and demanding in my shit. I fucked the shit out of him that night.

About two days later me and Blacc was laying up in the bed, when I heard a knock at my door, my little cousin Kita answered it, then I heard it close and music echo from the downstairs parking garage.

I asked her who it was, and she said *"Dre"*. Damn, I had to go tell him something as I ran after him. Dre finally stop the car; I confessed my truth.

I know I hurt his heart, but I had to be honest with him and myself, about me and Blacc's situation. Although I wasn't sure it was going anywhere, but that's something I needed to figure out. I didn't want to hinder him on finding someone that could give him what he needed, knowing I wasn't her at this point in my life. Dre hugged me tight and whispered in my ear *"He will always be waiting when I was ready"*. As I walk back upstairs, I was praying to God I didn't make another mistake with my choice of happiness

Chapter 10

Are we in a relationship?

My grandmother eventually was released from the hospital after her near-death experience. Although I stayed in Inglewood and only had a one-bedroom apartment it was better financially if we moved into her apartment, she had section 8 and her rent was way cheaper than mines.

Soon after my grandmother was released Blacc told me that he was leaving to go out of town, this time he finally gave me notice to when he was leaving but failed to decline his return date, typical.

After a few weeks and no correspondence, I figured he was gone completely, never in my wildest dreams did I think he was returning to me so soon, given his track record.

About two months passed and I concluded that he wasn't returning, well at least not back to me. I decided to take on the idea that it was what it was, friends with benefits again, this time no love was lost. I didn't feel abandoned or used.

I expected nothing more than what he was giving me. This time around I felt good about his departure, not because he was gone but because I had a different thinking process and understanding that neither him nor me was committed to each other.

I didn't see a problem in dating other people now, I wait for his return or contact and I, yet I still didn't get any, therefore when Renae introduced me to her other homeboy Nell, I didn't feel like I was cheating on anyone.

Nell and I talk awhile before we went out.

Nell was six two, about two hundred and twenty pounds, slender, nice teeth, very well groomed, and chocolate, not as dark as I like them, but his skin was still flawless because of his race.

Nell's demeanor was much different that some guys I dated, although you could see he had a lot of thug ways, and was street raised, you could also see that he had a different suave about himself, he dress real neat, fresh haircuts, he was responsible and planned things before he approached them, he had a goal in life and it didn't consist of him only selling pounds.

Nell and I relationship were fun, we went out on dates, stayed at home watch movies and chilled, he would do little things like have teddy bears and flowers waiting for me when I got to him place.

I could tell we were building something together; our potential friendship wasn't rushed or complicated with unknown agendas.

I found a bigger house for my grandmother to be comfortable in, which was convenient I didn't have to move her heavy furniture too far; you know that old school slave wood be heavy as fuck to move around the house let alone to a different location.

I rented a two-bedroom house right around the corner from where she already stayed, also closer to my daughter's school.

On the day that I was moving her belonging to the new house, Blacc walks in the apartment front door. Was I excited to see him? Yes, but damn every time I move on with my life without him, he finds a way to come back. I'm at the point of just telling him I can't! I can't be your stand in when you want to be my friend.

I can't be your play pretend women when you miss my sex, you can't keep leading me in directions towards going forward together, and then just fall off the face of the earth. The voice inside was saying all these things but my outside voice was occupied with his tongue down my throat.

Oh, how I missed him, his touch, his arms of embrace, but ole boy, why did I miss him so much, I thought as he was holding me tight.

Why did he have a control over me that directed my feeling? The more he held me the more I forgot I was in a monogamous relationship with Nell. Blacc laid me down on the bare floor of my grandmother's empty apartment and bless my body with his.

We were in this empty apartment making love, and that annoying nigga Tyrone was banging at the door. I forgot I had asked him to come help me move this stuff. Blacc didn't stop what he was doing until he was finished; about time our freak session ended Tyrone was gone, good.

I don't know what Blacc intention was with me that day, and I honestly didn't care, I was in the presence of the man I couldn't shake. I'm back feeling him.

From the first day we completely moved into this new house, Blacc was there nightly, he damn near lived there. Were my prayers of having him all to myself finally here?

Right now, I can say that we were together in a relationship, and not a commitment wasn't formed, but I figured we were.

Blacc slept in my bed every night, and woke up to me each morning, he brushed his teeth was washed his ass there, he even had some clothes hanging up in the closet, so was I wrong to think he was my man, nope.

At first Blacc didn't have a problem with how the house was ran or kept, then Blacc would start complaining about why the kitchen wasn't clean, dishes everywhere, why I always had to make the bed in order for him to go to sleep, and how I kept a lot of clothes on my closet floor, was I messy, yelp, but it wasn't like that all the time, but eight times out of ten was bad enough for him to make a big deal out of.

My body wasn't producing enough energy, come to find out I had blood disorder called Thalassemia which is unusual for

African Americans to get. I had severe anemia to the point where I need several blood transfusions, I was losing my own personal health battles while trying to keep my grandmothers going.

Blacc even started complaining about my whereabouts during the daytime. I used to like to hang in Gardena at my aunty house, and majority of the time I left my grandmother at home, not to long but long enough for me to get a mental break, from being nurse betty, all the fucking time, I needed to still feel young and not an old ass lady.

The caretaking of my grandmother was becoming stressful, I was able to do it but at times it was too demanding, I was only twenty-four years old, I was just relearning responsibility. I knew that what I was doing was the right and honorable thing to do, but it still felt overwhelming.

When I vanished Blacc would always find out where I was, I wasn't feeling this relationship thang, but he was starting to work my last nerves on him demands, he needed help he was a control freak.

When he would get to where I was I would use excuses like my gas was low, or I was doing something for my aunt, and Blacc would either give me the money to get back home, but he always talk shit in the process, not the shit talking where you are a sack of lazy bitches, but the shit talking like I knew better and should be doing better.

After hearing his voice repeatedly, I finally got some act right, truth be told it was his voice that made me do right it was that good dick he gave me when I did.

Over the course of the last eight years I kept in contact with my old boyfriend Malik family, so when he called me out the blue, I was surprised but I knew that this day was approaching fast, he will be released on January eleventh nineteen ninety seven. I had to decide to see him somehow.

Blacc would leave daily to do his street running whether it was hustling or banging, we never disclosed that side of each other to each other, but whatever it was that he did I knew he would be gone for a few hours so I can sneak away to see Malik's face.

Chapter 11

Can you come pick me up?

A few days before Malik was going to be released from jail,

Blacc left for a few hours and returned home, with a baby girl in his arms, I immediately thought that the baby was one of his sister's kids he was watching, because her and him shared familiar facial similarities, then Blacc drop the bomb on me when he said she belong to him, now this baby has to be about three to four months old, and three or four months ago we were here, not only that but before that nine months prior we were at my house in Inglewood where he was ordering me to put people out my house. Damn, my heart drop.

I knew about his first daughter, her and my daughter shared the same birthday, also he told me about his other son, but he never told me anything about this baby or being involved with any other females I know we are not committed, but the nigga couldn't even keep it one hundred. As I held this chocolate little girl, I imagine me holding shy, it was bittersweet.

After finding out about this child that he hid, again I felt cheated, all these women were allowed to carry one of his children without doubt they wouldn't be by themselves, me on the other end only wish my hole nine months he showed any possibility of any future together.

I didn't act any different with his baby, matter of fact I like the fact that he included me in her life with him, but I somewhat resented his behavior, he took my options away long before I knew I had any, by him covering up the fact that it was a young lady who might potentially be the mother to one your children, then when you found out the kid was yours you declined to share it with the women you lay next to each night. I thought he had a little more respect for us as friends and lovers.

On account of his betrayal I really decided to go see Malik and leave the possibility of me and him open, why should I continue to put my all in someone who openly violated our unprotected unity and then selfishly hid the fact that you fathered a child with someone other than me?

I went over to see Malik and the only reason why I didn't have sex with him was because I was on my period, but on the seventeenth I was in his bed, not thinking about Blacc, sad part was I didn't even enjoy it, it was quick, and his dick was little as fuck. I didn't even know that Malik came inside me, until I went to stand up and semen drip out my vagina and saw the unopened Trojan on his nightstand.

Was I scared of diseases, no, he was fresh out the penitentiary, and I wasn't worried about pregnancy because the correctional facility give inmate sweet Peter, the juice that decreased males sexual urges, and if that wasn't enough I had been on the depo shot since my daughter was four years old, so I had no worries when we fuck unprotected.

So afterwards, I called Blacc and ask him to come get me from Malik house, I know that was some hoe Shit, but I need to add salt his sugar.

The next day me and Blacc were at the house along, and sometimes when we were a lone we would fuck like dogs, all over the house, but this time it was different, we passionately fucked like crazy, in front of the open windows, curtains pulled back, me on top of my grandmother passed down wooden dinette table inside the formal living room, on the floor, him walking around carrying me, and when he came I felt him becoming one with me, we were whole, he was mine again.

Chapter 12

My answer will always be the same

54

Everything in my life is going as good as expected my grandmother's health was improving, me and Blacc was on better terms, and it appeared that we both were finally seeing eye to eye on the u's situation.

As normal I would go get my depo shot, and this time I was telling Dr Jefferson that I felt my blood was low, because I be having major headaches and feeling weak like I did before I was diagnosed with the blood disorder. Dr. Jefferson said he will take some blood samples to see if I need another transfusion or iron infusion; the office will contact me about an update as soon as the results come back in.

I often spoke with that nigga Tyrone, as he was holding a secret that could have sent mentor the federal prison so, I always tried to make sure he was alright and doing well, he could have easily told my part in the operation, but for some reason his loyalty to me was more valuable then another name in other people's paperwork.

Therefore, I felt obligated at times to be attentive to his small demands of attention, it was never sexual just a listening ear and a few dollars every now and again.

Blacc never knew hustling side of me, and I don't think it would have been good at any time to disclose things I did, although we shared intimate details of each other's pass it was something that's felt he wouldn't have understood or might have thought differently about me, like if I was going to ever try him one day, in didn't need him to ever have to question the reason or reasons I was with him. He was never my prey, I loved him.

While I was on the phone with Tyrone an unknown caller called, I click over answered the phone and it was the Dr. Jefferson's office, "Miss Jackson", 'Yes'. I said, we have the results from the lab.

"*Congratulations you are pregnant, we need to schedule a prenatal appointment with you to begin care, is Feb 23rd. good for you?*" I said "*Wait, I'm pregnant, how?, I'm on the shot*", the receptionist said, "*Sometimes our bodies get use to the injections and it does the opposite, and in your case it made you more fertile instead of prevention*". I don't recall the remainder or the call, I click back over, Tyrone ask was I okay and I just started crying uncontrollably, but he kept asking what's wrong.

Tyrone and I was always friends, even though he had stalkers tendencies, but somehow I felt I could share with him, he was also a person I considered to be a true friend.

I said "*Tyrone, nigga I'm pregnant by this nigga Blacc again*", I think the news of me having someone else's baby hurt his feeling, and he hung up in my face. I wasn't worried about what Tyrone thought; my biggest concern was how Blacc was going to receive this notice.

About two weeks pass, and even though we slept in the same bed, I was scared to tell him. One morning he got up and left and returned with his little girl, now I might be able to slide the conversation of my baby with him.

We all were laying down taking a nap and I mention how nice this would be if it was our baby laying here instead of him and another women's.

I don't think he really entertained what ideas saying right then, because he brushed off my whole conversation by saying Stacy go to sleep.

Another week passed and now I'm having morning sickness, and could barely do anything, so again we're having conversations about keeping this house clean. So, I tell him, I'm pregnant; Blacc tells me he didn't want any more kids. I think I lost respect for him at that moment.

In my head I'm thinking he could get all these random bitches pregnant, bring their babies up in my face, and expect me to be okay with that. What made them more worthy than me to carry his kid?

I knew when he said those words that it was the end of US. God was giving us both an opportunity to correct a mistake from years ago, and he want me to kill this kid too. I didn't have the heart to face another questionable sin of God's.

As the weeks came and left, so did Blacc, he wasn't really there at the house anymore, he would seldom come pass look in and check on my grandmother and if I was there we might say few words to each other but nothing was serious but the question he kept asking as my stomach grew bigger, you really going to keep this baby, and my answer will always be the same, Yep, this my kid.

One day Blacc left and I seen him for about a month or so later, so again I figured he was gone again like he always did.

Tyrone needed a place to stay, why he couldn't go over his mama house, is unknowing to me, but my grandmother said it was okay for him to stay.

While Tyrone was there in our home, unwanted, he did everything I asked like a personal slave, he knew damn well I didn't want him there at all; he slept in the living room on the couch also took my daughter to school each day, cleaned my house, took care of my grandmother when I needed a break.

I recall being about sixteen weeks along and my front doorbell rung, my grandmother called out someone's at the door, and before I could get to it Blacc walk right in, who invited him?

Blacc took a seat on the couch, started conversations with my grandmother, I walk in my room and closed the door, and we had nothing to say to each other, I was done.

When he didn't chase behind me, I decided to find a reason to see his face again, so I went and stood over the floor heater that had been on since the day we moved in January.

I'm looking at Blacc in my proverbial vision, Blacc face turned really awkward and really strange when Tyrone walk outside kitchen into the living room, to make matter worse this fool Tyrone stands right behind me on this heater and puts his hand on my stomach, what the fuck he do that for?

That's when all hell broke loose, Blacc jump up and convince to beating the dog shit out of Tyrone, low-key I was happy he was getting fucked up, why would he do that in the first place, you not my man, nor was we fucking, you was just staying at our house because I felt obligated to do so, all the times your mom and sisters let me and my son stay-at theirs and because you snitched on all the homie and they was doing time and you didn't tell on me. But that was some bitch shit he just did.

My grandmother on the other hand was trying to get Blacc off Tyrone ass, I told her *"Mama let them fight"*, she said *"he gone kill him, he gone kill him"*. When Blacc got tired he stops.

That's the day Tyrone had to leave my house immediately. As I look at all stuff scattered in the living room, like hurricane Blacc was here, I couldn't help but ask was he okay, he told me not to say Shit to him and walk out the door. About an hour pass and here he came pulling up in the driveway, first thing he ask, was if I was okay, as watched him get out his car, and walk towards me, he hug me tight then went in to explained why things transpired to my grandmother, him and her always had a family connection.

Needless we was right back doing us, waking up and going

sleep. Out the blue one day Tyrone called and told me that he was watching me and Blacc sleep at night and that sometimes he sneaks in our house and see us in our bed making love I started to tell Blacc about the things that Tyrone would say on the phone so therefore Blacc made sure that it was a gun in my room and in his car when he drove up just for our protection.

I didn't know if the things Tyrone was saying was true or not, but it was always good to make my man aware of the potential hazard.

One night when Blacc came home Tyrone approached his car like a smoker, and started to tell Blacc are sort of lies and yelling things out like why are you with her she has AIDS, she's going to dog you out, I'm paid hoe, and all kind of weird stuff and Blacc really didn't pay him no attention, I kind of laugh when Tyrone called Blacc, Biggie Smalls I thought that was funny, being my dude was getting on the thick side and was black as hell.

Tyrone became a full-blown stalker to the point where he was really dangerous I was really afraid that he might do something to me because of my dealings with Blacc, he was unstable and he had nowhere to go and he felt he lost his friend so either he was going to kill me or report to the police either way he couldn't be trusted.

Chapter 13

Repent while they still here

We had some strange people to move in the house behind ours, I call them the street walkers, running in and out the front gate, like smokers do.

It was the beginning of the second week of May 1998, and me, my grandmother and Blacc was on the front porch, and the smoker dude from the back said some slick shit to Blacc about his car taking over the driveway, now in Blacc defense it shouldn't have been an issue, they didn't even have a car, so why would a driveway be important to some walking motherfuckers.

Blacc was a person you just didn't want to rub the wrong way or appear to be about that gangster life if you weren't. Blacc was the type to slap the bitch out a nigga. Any nigga would have been better off shooting Blacc verse trying to use their hands. Situations like that was a no win.

I begged Blacc to leave, because I didn't want him to knock this nigga out or be place in a situation where he had to shoot this stupid ass nigga, because I knew he would snitch and send my baby daddy to jail.

Blacc and I just got to the point where he was low-key accepting this pregnancy and the fact that I was carrying the baby.

On May 15th, the same dude was pacing up and down the driveway, yelling profanity, it was becoming a nuisance to grandmother, she slowly walks outside and ask the fellow to calm down, and he started cursing my grandmother out real crazy like.

I had enough of this bitch ass nigga unstable ass ways. I went out in the porch area, waited for this dude to walk towards his adjacent house, swung open the back door, I grab our Rottweiler dog chain off the ground and when he walk pass me

I started beating him with that metal chain, the dude instantly feel on the ground.

I thought I knock him out them, but then he started bellowing so loudly our neighbors started coming out looking across the gated fence. I don't know what came over me, but I kept hitting him and hitting him, until someone grab my arm, by this time old boy was out cold and bleeding.

My next-door neighbor Frank grab the chain and took it to his house, I went on the inside mines while old boy's women tried to wake him up. Approximately fifteen minutes passed and the whole 77th police department was in my front yard, banging on my front door.

First, I wasn't going to answer it, I was going to pretend nobody was home, then I thought fuck it, I might as well go to jail. That's how pissed I was. Before I could open the door, I called over to Tyrone mama's house and told who ever answered the phone to come get Christina and my grandmother; I was on my way to jail.

I was arrested on assault and battery charges and booked at 77th police department; my Stepmom asked if I wanted her to post bail after she told me my grandmother ended up at the hospital later that night. I told her nope, I will sit here. I was still mad as hell and too stubborn to get out.

On day two a detective finally came and questioned me, I gave the statement of "*I don't know what happen to cuz, I was in my house sleep*" and that was my story.

I can't tell on myself, and none of my neighbors did either, it was my word against his, I had no visual marks on my hands, and I stressed the idea that I was pregnant and all that trauma they said was done to him, could not have been done by me. I'm little, it was remotely impossible for someone my size and stature to cause such damage with my hands.

They never found the chain he claimed I used; therefore, I was released before my seventy-two hours was up.

As I walk home, I kept saying how I'd missed Mother's Day, and that I hope my grandmother was home.

When I returned to the house, she opens the door, man I was so happy to be out. I gave my grandmother her gifts, sat up for a minute, and then I went and wash 77th PD off me.

About time I got out the tub, my grandmother was having trouble breathing, which caused her to have to be rushed to the hospital. That was May 20th, she died on May 21st and I buried her on May 27th, 1998.

Chapter 14

Second time around

The day after my grandmother died, I remember sitting on her front porch staring into nowhere. All I could do was cry. I felt like the loneliest person in this world. I had nobody but my little girl and my unborn daughter.

My family was near but far. I would watch the people walk down the street and just look at me and shake their heads in sadness and all I kept thinking is that they know I was headed for a world of hurt.

I close my eyes and I used to think of all the good times, all the bad times, and the last time I saw her face. As the traffic echoed up and down our block, I recall looking outward and seeing Blacc as he drove up in the driveway.

Blacc got out of his car and as he was walking towards me, Blacc asked me where is Mama?, and I just looked at him dumbfounded somewhat in a blank stare he asked me again, and he just went straight in the house, he walked back out and aggressively asked again, and that when I had the voice to tell him I buried her yesterday.

Blacc kneeled next to me and just hugged me, and with my head skunked in his chest I cried till I couldn't cry no more. The more I released the more he held me tighter. As much as I miss him and his embrace his comfort didn't make me feel better, I was lost.

Every day after my grandmother's funeral, I would just go to her house and sit on the front porch, something in me was scared to go inside that house.

I had nightly dreams that she was in her room lying in her bed, with her eye wide open, waiting on me to come back there, and once I got near her bedside, she would pop up, and then I would wake up.

I know my mind was playing tricks on me, I was becoming unstable and reckless, I forgot what sleep was, food was something I smelled and never tasted, Newport's and Pepsi became my best friend.

My comfort was nestled in the ground at somebody cemetery, where was my go-to now. I need something to help me deal with a lot of misunderstanding that life was throwing in my direction. Have you ever been so distraught that you forget night and day?

I was hurting so bad on the inside and not the pain you feel when you fall and scrape your knee, but a pain Blacc escapades never bestowed on me, a pain on emptiness, a feeling of lost, you know when you cry and you feel it way down in your soul and that begins to hurt.

I didn't want to be around anyone, I was a walking zombie, the pain where you have nobody left in the world and your eyes fill up with tears and you try so hard to see but everything in your vision is blurred and unreadable.

I was losing my mind, I needed immediate professional help.

I was alone, and lonely. I don't know if during that time I was pushing Blacc away, I understand he was giving me some time. Blacc knew firsthand the history me and my grandmother had.

Months after her death I was getting me back, I found a job at brinks on the money truck as an armed guard; anything was good to keep my mind occupied.

Eventually I moved far away from my grandmother house, into a one-bedroom apartment. I had talk with Blacc a few times, but we hadn't had sex in months.

I wasn't tripping he had someone else, at that time in my life I didn't even want him anymore, I just wanted my grandmother to come back or take me with her.

My heart was out of love, and tired of hurt. I was so thru chasing him and what he never offered in exchanged for me.

I had my little girl and I recall the day that I went into labor, it crazy that during all the years we known each other Blacc may not have always been around when I needed him, but he was always there when his time was needed.

Blacc paged me and he asked, *"Where I was?"* I told him *"Over to my aunt's house"* he then said *"Well I'm on my way over there"* I replied *"No you not! I'm going to go home in a minute"* I haven't been out the delivery room a good ten minutes before that page, he knew.

I went home the next day after I had my daughter and I wasn't really tripping then it was a knock at my door, I'm thinking maybe one of my neighbors had heard I had the baby and was trying to come see her, everyone in my building knew I lived alone with my daughter and was pregnant with no baby daddy, they saw me daily.

When I open the door, it was Blacc and he took the baby out my arms when I open the door, I couldn't deny her to him, but how dare he interrupt my peace. Remember he didn't want her at first, now he's so in love. I couldn't figure how that was even remotely possible, what did he want?

Blacc mention how beautiful she was and how much she resembled him, he stay a few hours, asking me random ass questions nothing related to my baby or my ability to provide for her, he was basically trying to see if I was fucking anybody and bull shit like that.

Although I had recently had a baby, didn't stop me from being sexually deprived. My body ached to be touched by the opposite sex.

Blacc and I hooked up sexually a few times before my daughter was six weeks old, call it being nasty, I called it taking care of my stability.

Besides I didn't think nothing of it you know after you have a baby sometimes you have a missed period or two sometimes it needs time to get back on track, but it was devastating to find out at my six weeks checkup I was four weeks pregnant.

Bout time my daughter was three months old I was two months pregnant. Blacc was aware of the pregnancy and said that I needed to terminate it soon as possible, but that wasn't a decision he needed to decide.

I never ask him for any assistance with my baby. So why would I need his help with anymore, but eventually I knew I need to decide fast, my days were getting fewer.

I thought about all kinds of alternatives such as adoption, but couldn't carry another edition of me and watch while someone else walks away with my kid, and then it was abortion, although I have heard good and bad stories, at the age of twenty four I had one other one prior.

Once I made the decision to have abortion, Blacc was in agreement, I think his motives for that choice was to keep his girlfriend happy, and my reasons was I needed to be happy, and less stress, and I really couldn't stomach even mothering anymore of his children.

I wouldn't say I hated Blacc, but I was developing a strong dislike towards him, he just wasn't the same dude I feel overly in love with years ago, too much transpired between us, and the bad outweighed the good.

One day before my procedure I paged him, and this girl called me back, this was new, I don't care who or where he was in his life, Blacc never been that careless to have women confront me about US, this was an all-time low.

As the lady talk, she explained her and his relationship, she told me they already had a child together and was expecting twins soon, and so on and on, I think I stop breathing when we said more children and they were together as a couple.

I knew who the first child was, that little chocolate baby I use to watch, but now more babies, by the same women, he must have had a different type of love other than any he ever expressed with me.

I allowed my hurt to take control of the conversation with ole girl, words were exchanged, promises of me beating her ass were talk about, but even after all that she still had something I didn't, Him.

Once ole girl confronted him with me, Blacc called and I'm sure I did the same, even after he tried to tell me they relationship was just two people drunk fucking, I believed he would lie to me to keep me around for his personal fee fee bag. I'm sure my conversation was more verbal and hurtful; I demanded that he come with me to get this procedure done, and I would be finally free of him completely. I was tired of not being his only one, fuck him, how dare he continue to treat me like shit, fuck him.

The day I was scheduled to go to the abortion clinic, Blacc didn't return any of my calls, he didn't come over he didn't come up to the doctor's office he did nothing.

I was already beating myself up back and forth because I had experienced this before, and I was scared. But nevertheless, it seems like the only option I had at that time.

The clinic reassured me that the process will be smooth and safely performed, yeah right, I was never given an ultrasound to tell them how many fetuses I was carrying nor, an indication of the exact due date, the whole ordeal was carried out careless and unprofessional.

During the termination process of removing the fetuses from my body they only remove one when in fact I was carrying twins, so they must do the whole process over again and that mentally put me in a distraught situation.

I was again reliving the death of Shy, the death of Kurt's unborn child, the death of my grandmother, and the evil death my babies suffered. For days after all I thought was, I killed my daughter by being very selfish and not thinking of her well-being, and here I was four years later, taking the life of my babies because I was unstable.

I needed to find peace, I need a medium in my life, I needed to break free of the one man that caused so much heartache and dysfunction in my life, I needed to relieve myself of Blacc completely without hesitation, at that time in my life, My hinder was destroying my happiness.

Chapter 15

41ˢᵗ. Drive

I moved out of that apartment soon as I was well enough to maneuver and find a place where I couldn't be found, somewhere wouldn't nobody look for me at, my stepmoms. I felt into be the safest place around being that our relationship was estranged, Blacc would never look for me here.

I started back having drinks to ease my mind, it help me gather my thoughts, first it started one here one there, then I was full fledge drinking every night, it was my happy, the more I drank the more I was losing my thought process.

Don't get it twisted I only drink at night, and I never drank alone, I always had a squad of people around, my lil cousin or some of the homies, that was our out. Out of mind and out of sight. I found my medium in the bottom of a Paul Mason bottle.

It was a few dudes that lived on the same block, but I never took anyone of them serious, they were all handsome, but they curbed served.

That was a no no, it was almost the year two thousand and they still making eighty-six money. My lifestyle wouldn't have met the budgets, I was back looking for my next come up, I got mouths to feed, and need a place to go.

When I would go outside and chill on the front porch as my son made his rounds in the neighborhood, I would watch how the dudes all watch me. As I walk my son to the corner store, or when I got my kids in and out my car, they watch. I know that I was cute, but they all look like some thirsty dogs looking for a bitch.

One day one of the dudes came across the street and spoke, I look at him coldly, and said "What's up". I didn't know if these fools were my enemy or not, I lived in somebody else hood, then he asked for a cigarette, tried to hold small talk and I curved his ass.

The next day the same fellow made his way back over on my side of the street, and gave me a cigarette, now I thought this gesture was pretty noble, maybe he not a bum after all, as I got in my car to go get a pint of mason and come back to my car and listen to "I miss You" by Teddy Pendergrass on repeat.

Every morning the same dude would be outside smoking weed, I know people smoke but it like six-thirty in the morning, dame my nigga, did you even brush or wash your face before you rolled up.

When I came back home from dropping my son off to school he would still be outside now doing something to his car, he had a little bucket so it might have needed some work each day, which he made sure he park right in front of our house. I was starting to think he was a stalker.

I knew dude must have been attractive to me, because every time I look in his direction, he would be smiling back at me. No doubt dude was handsome, but he wasn't my typical type of dude that I would date. Dude was muscular, had a reddish brown tint complexion, you can tell he not too long ago got out of county jail or state penitentiary, face was clean shaven, fresh haircut, name brand attire, decent shoes, and I could tell when he smiled he had pretty white teeth, but his pockets wasn't my type,   Broke.

I decided to walk up to his car one day and asked what his name was, he told me his name was Harold. I said *"Harold yeah you look like you your mother had named Harold"* he said *"Why you say that"* I responded *"I didn't mean any disrespect but sometimes people names fit them,"* he said *" what's yours"*, I replied *"Stacy"*, he said *"Yeah you look like a Stacy, no disrespect."*

First time in a long time I smiled. I turned and began to walk away, he yelled *"Aye Stacy aye you want to hit my blunt"*, I yelled back, *"Naw I don't smoke, and walk in my house"*.

From that day forward Harold made it his business to speak, when I took my daughter to school and when I came from picking her up. On account of his persistence, we then formed a neighborly friendship.

Found out he was from the same hood I was, and to make a connection when I was younger, we use to play with each other, who would have thought Harold was the boy next door.

Harold homeboys and my homegirls would all kick it outside in the middle of the night or upstairs in his homeboy Mikes apartment, just laughing, and drinking, everyone was cool with each other.

My homegirls didn't have any intentions of dating any of them but the guys sure cater to girls with hope that someone would, Harold and I used to sit back and plot on our friends about who was going to hook up first out the crew, never did I think it would have been us.

I didn't intentional seek a relationship with Harold, but he became my ear to go to, he listen to all the things I had to say about Blacc, he watch me cry many nights wondering why I couldn't find love, over time Harold just grew on me mentally, he was the friend of the girl who heart was broken by another man, he knew what not to do to get me.

Did he have hidden motives? Unknown.

After several months of us chilling in each other's company I felt I was ready to take our relationship to the next level. Our getaway to transfer our friendship to a relationship was watch by our entire block.

Not watch as in a porn episode, but everyone knew that Harold and I had never been intimate with each other yet, matter of fact his boys used to tease him because he hadn't got it yet, some of them even had a money wager of the timeframe it would take him to lay me down, I guess that something that men do.

The day came for us to spend the night together; we didn't tell any of our friends our plans, when night fell, we both just slipped away. Harold got us a hotel room, we had some Paul Mason, he had his weed, and I had the condoms.

Sex with him was different, like inexperienced, he had a nice package but he didn't know how to maneuver with some pussy, sex wasn't trash at all, he knew how to eat the pussy not as good as Blacc, he could have been better in the positions. I will teach him next time.

I was used to getting and being fucked. I'm sure I fucked his mind just as much as I fucked his body. Hasn't had sex with a man in over six months so he works what needed to be work on.

I hadn't saw black in almost six months, I made sure I changed my pager number, and told anybody that had mutual contact with him, to say they didn't know where I was, I wipe him out my internal memory when I gave Harold listening ears my cleansing of him.

One day me and my baby girl was having a small picnic outside on the front lawn, as she played in her bouncer, she was only seven months old at the time, but she like to go outside and for the grass to tickle her little feet, all the homies was sitting across the street, and my baby was in plain view of them, I yelled *"Aye watch her while I run in the house real quick"* they all agreed.

The most shocking thing happen when I went into the house, apparently Blacc saw the baby sitting outside, in his quest to find me, when I open the front door; he had our little girl in his arms. How did he find me?

I was starting to feel that Blacc had some type of tracking device on my heart, when I find someone I felt comfortable to share with, he always found a way to come in between, but this time, I really did like Harold and I knew Harold like me more. My heart was in love, a love that was not sexual, but a love that was honest and illustrated.

Blacc saw the dude across the street staring at him, as he parked his low rider across my mama green grass, this fool even pancake the two door cutlass, he was such a naive show off, but that's the type of shit I liked about Blacc, even when he didn't do the extras he made me want him more, but because the homies was staring and looking sideways, Blacc made it a point to address me with it.

One thing he hated is when people eye fucked him, he immediately *said "Which one of them niggas you are fucking"* I said *"None",* and I was telling the truth, Harold wasn't over there at that time.

Blacc stayed about an hour we both had short talk for each other, basic and general conversations, and no we didn't talk about us, we didn't talk about sex, I only talk when he asked a question.

I was still trying to figure out his motives for this surprise visit. Before he left, we didn't make in commitment to keep in touch, Blacc just told me to call him if our daughter needs anything, I was fine with that, and it was what it was.

My baby was always good, I didn't need to call on Blacc for shit. I never told Malik she wasn't or was his, he just assumed, and I kept it that way.

My baby always went over Malik house to visit, stay the nights, his family loved my baby. I maliciously removed Blacc from her life, when his bitch calls me back that day, he only had one time to ever cross me with one of his bitches.

Blacc didn't need my baby he was out making himself a family with a random. My daughter was never going be a side kid to anyone, she deserved a father that was not going to hide her, or fuck with her when he wanted too, not mines.

About three months into our new relationship Harold and I end up moving into an apartment together and that's when my happiness became my hinder. Haven't heard from Blacc in a few months, then one day I was out shoe shopping and this nigga walks right past me, so I say.

You not going to fucking speak; he turns in my direction and looks spooked. I thinking he was high, but he tells me to follow him down a bit, he sits down acting like he is putting a pair of shoes on and whisper the Feds are watching him.

I look around, really thinking cuz is super high, "*Okay*" I say, in disbelief, I had several pair of shoes in my hands for the kids, he takes them out my arms, walks over to the cashier and buys them, he hands me a hand full of money and his cell number, then walks away, after he tells me to buy my dude some shoes too, that was Blacc's was of being funny and sarcastic. That made me feel a little warm inside, he lowkey tripping I'm with someone else.

Since that day forward Blacc and I would get together, he kept me fulfilled sexually, while Harold did mentally. I'm winning I got my cake and I'm eating it too. Was I becoming the selfish lover, with no regards to my partner's feeling, yes, and I have no regrets?

I was committing emotional infidelity. Can a person be in love with two people, "*Yes*", the love is not the same; I loved both these men differently. One I found security in and the other was my mental security. One heart equally divided between the two, it was complicated and exciting at the same time.

After a few months of my mindless behavior I found out I was again pregnant, I had to make a choice of security. This was the first time Blacc didn't demand that I was an abortion, maybe because I didn't know who belong to, but I was keeping it.

The more I got bigger the more Blacc kept asking if it was his, truth be told I don't know who the father was, if the dates match up of my date of conceiving, then I would be lost, I had sex with two men on the same day.

I would never tell Blacc that it was his, and I never told Harold I didn't think it wasn't his. Seems as though I had a problematic track record of not being for sure of my children's father.

My little cousin and I got into it, she got so mad at me that the tramp told Harold when he got off to work for weeks at a time, and I would have Blacc at my house. I didn't want to make it seem like she was telling the truth, so I let her talk, then she went on to say, that she caught me sucking Blacc dick one night she walk in my room, and that my baby was Blacc's and not his, Harold look at me really strange, like he was going to choke the life out of me, and that when enough was enough and I knock her off cold in my living room.

I was nine months pregnant, now people are beginning to become reckless with the mouth, I couldn't wait on the next person to feel the need to expose me. Harold still never questions my baby paternity.

On count of Blacc in and off of my life, I had no choice but to run again, if my child was his, I would be a mother whose age is twenty five with three kids and no daddy around, on the other hand Harold wasn't going nowhere and was excited I was having his son.

A week before I delivered my son, I moved to Palmdale, out there Blacc wouldn't come look, and hinder was trying to impose on my happiness.

Chapter 16

Loving two is different than loving one

I was almost my little girls birthday, and me and my lil cousin were out shopping, then I remember that Blacc had a sister that worked for JC Penny's inside the mall, maybe I could get her employees discount on some things for the baby, I thought as I walked in. That was the first time someone in his family ever saw my baby.

After shopping I had to go to work myself, I work three jobs, one full-time at Macy's, and two parties at Leather mode and the gap store inside the southeast galleria, depending on my schedules on certain days dedicated the time I had to spend with Blacc.

While I was at work or with Blacc, Harold stayed home and kept my kids. No more street hustling, I really love him and didn't want him to get in any trouble out there in the streets doing wrong.

I took care of the house, although he sold weed out the apartment. Harold was presented with the offer to go fight fires for the forest service; it was good opportunity for him, and more money in his pockets.

Harold leaving all the time, gave me the chance to spend more time with Blacc, I knew what I was doing with Blacc was wrong, but I couldn't stop.

I enjoyed being around Blacc. I knew he was with someone, but didn't know who, and I didn't care, and I accepted any way he came, and it was always better when he came in me.

I would get highly upset if he hadn't come by and gave me my fix, I was truly addicted to this man, and his sex. Nobody has ever made me feel the way he have, it's not about the stock or position, it more complicated than that, it's the passion, knowing he wants me too, it's the security I feel when I'm with him, the years I vested loving this only man, it's the comfort he gives my heart when he holds me close, after all the things we went thru within our on again off again situation, and all the times I experienced heartache because he wasn't mine, but he was, when we were together and that's all I needed.

Was I becoming a selfish lover, with no regards to my partner? Can a person be in love with two people at the same time, Yes, one gave me security and the other was my security?

Could my greed for the affection of this one man ruin the unity I was establishing with another? Or was this a case of me having my cake and eating it too.

I think you call a person who has a divided heart a person who practices emotional infidelity. One heart that's equally divided between two men became complicated yet exciting.

About two months passed since Harold was a fully-fledged firefighter, and it was two months that I was regularly getting dick down in the bed I shared with my boyfriend.

I didn't think it was scandalous because before Harold purchased this mattress the one, he slept on before me and Blacc shared.

The day I found out I was pregnant I had to make some big girl decisions, first it was never a question in my mind if I

Was going to keep my baby, sure I was, I vowed to never have another abortion. And secondly, I didn't know who the baby belongs to, I found myself back in the same situation with my daughter almost two years ago.

As my stomach grew so did the questions from Blacc weather this child was his or not, to be honest this was the first time Blacc didn't demand me to have an abortion, perhaps he felt safe because the baby father was never identified. I never once told Blacc it was his, and never gave Harold any reasons to believe it wasn't his.

I knew that if the truth ever came out from Blacc being cocky and arrogant saying some slick shit with Harold it would hurt the one man that appeared to ever had wanted me more than I wanted him, Harold was a good dude to my kids, and I believe he would have made a decent father to all my children, so there it was my decision was made, before I face the truth I would run until the day the truth finds me.

About a week before I delivered my son, Blacc would never find me here. I would never be faced with having to hurt anyone feelings. Or placed in a situation where I was all alone, waiting on my baby daddy to come check up on us, when he felt like it.

Harold and I needed this child to keep our unity strong between us. All honesty I needed this baby to keep my happiness from being my hinder. I delivered my son on the Fourth of July two thousand.

Chapter 17

How I wish things could have been

It's been a few years since I spoke to Blacc, my daughter is about four and my son is two. I now have a total of four children, married and in a monogamous relationship.

We decided to move back to Los Angeles, closer to family and friends. I would often think about Blacc, hell I thought about him every day, every time I look in my baby girl's eyes, I saw him, she looks so much like him it was crazy, it was like a mini Blacc.

Out the blue on day I made a call to his sister Monica, I kind of wanted to know if he was still alive, Naw, I needed to see him, not for sex but just because, he was still my friend, although it was years since we last spoke, I need to hear his voice, even if it was just over the phone, I gave her my number she told me she would pass it alone, when she saw him.

Less than a day, I got the call I needed, Blacc, he asked about our daughter, didn't say too much about my son, we agreed to meet, he stayed in Victorville, which wasn't that far from where I was, the next day I was off to see him.

When I got to his house, I observed baby toys over the living room area, I'm thinking he got little kids that live in this home with him, he told me to come in his room, he laid across his bed, I sat on the side up right, I didn't feel comfortable, his home look occupied, like he established himself a family.

Blacc wanted to have sex, and every piece of me turned down the offer, as much as I wanted his body inside of mines, as many times I dreamed this day would happen again, I couldn't no longer bestow the hurt of infidelity upon another women, as I was just getting pass an ordeal like that with my own husband.

Blacc and I shared about the things we went thru apart, and laugh, and just chilled, I kept asking him when his family was going to return, he never answered my question.

This time Blacc was my ear, I told him about how my husband was mistreating me with his cheating, and other issues we were having, Blacc mention the idea of me coming to live out there with him.

I thought he was just talking out the side of his head, I didn't even think twice, but that idea, the way his home was set up he already had more than he could handle, family guy.

Blacc took my daughter shopping, we had lunch at his place, and then I jump back on the freeway to awaiting family. That night I cried in the bathroom as I took a shower, I cried because I was missing something in my life, I cried because the one man I love and has always love was taken, not just having a girlfriend, but he was taken his life was with another, she gave him something he never wanted from me a family.

I cried on the what if's, and I should have different, and the possibilities of, I cried because I was in a marriage I made to escape a man I couldn't get to love me the way I love him in return, I cried because I was so unhappy in the choices I made in life, I cried because Blacc had a full life outside of me, I cried because I wasn't her and my kids wasn't them. They say don't go looking, if you not ready to see.

Shortly after that I felt the need to leave again so somewhere new, change up my atmosphere, get as many miles away from him, it was bad when I didn't know where he was, but now I do, and the hurt of not being able to walk on his front porch and confess my love, without him laughing uncontrollably in my face, ate at my soul.

Blacc didn't want me, and at this point was my reality that we never had anything, I imagined it all in my head, I was his personal stocker, if he ever wanted need the way I wanted him I would or we would be together, sad case of reality.

I moved to Las Vegas, Nevada, and hope this change would bring on a difference in my make-believe happiness. One day I called Blacc sister house, that's how I was always able to keep in touch with him, and his baby mama answered, the same one when I was pregnant and again this bitch gave me an ear full, about their family, how many children they had, and so on and so forth, and because she was filling my head and heart with all these things.

I believed to be true, I entertained her conversation, he grabs the phone from her Blacc told me to never call him again, good by bitch he said when he hung up in my face, my friend was gone.

I became depressed to the point where I would sleep all the time, I would sneak and cry when everyone was sleep, I would hold my daughter and tell her I was all she ever needed, I stop combing my hair, didn't leave my house too often, my depression was consuming me.

It didn't all have to do with getting rejected by Blacc it was just my life was depressing, I already had six kids and the last two I didn't even recall making. Harold was cheating left and right and I was having babies back to back. Is this where my life was headed, if only I still could talk to my friend, the one person in my world that made me happy, just because.

Chapter 18

Only in my presence

Husband and I relationship were spiraling to hell. The more I lived in the city of wind, the weaker I was getting. My strength to live was a fantasy.

Somewhere in the last few years I lost my completely trying to find something that wasn't destined to be mines, stability, self-improvement and Blacc.

I decided to uproot my family back to familiar land, I needed to see more smiling faces of people I had love and respect for, long as Harold and I were away from everybody and everything he was comfortable, he didn't have to worry about my family or my homies getting on his head.

I needed my comfort zone again, even though Blacc will never be in my presence, at least I have the possibility to see him in traffic one day. Wishful thinking, I guess.

When I moved back to California, I went and stay at my aunts and Harold stayed with his uncle. That was the plan before I took off; we were not in a relationship anymore.

Harold came to my aunt house daily trying to get us back together, but at this point I was feeling our relationship to be at its end. I was no longer emotionally attached.

Harold vowed to change his ways and try and improve on our union. I needed help with my kids and felt I had no choice but to remain together unhappy. It was my fear of the unknown, not wanting to raise any of my children by myself, who would really consider dating a woman with as many kids as I had.

Harold became very jealous and clingy, but he treated me so awful and disrespectful to the point where I was starting to believe the things he said or did was my truth waiting to happen. I needed a change, something or somebody had to give.

Here I was back in California, this time I was going to do it right. My plan was to get myself together and walk away from the man that pretended to Love me. I wasn't going to let life drain the living out of me, I decided to start my own business and direct this unhealthy energy into a positive money flow, and that's just what I did.

I had one of the most growing businesses in the Antelope Valley. My brand was becoming a household name. I had contracts after contracts, bank account was full, my family was secure, and now my husband was happy and faithful.

It took for me to make a change, totally devote all my time and energy into becoming financially stable for my husband to decide he wanted me, bullshit, I was being taken on a ride, and the sad part is I knew, but inside I kept thinking who did I really had in my corner.

I use to think did me sinking in the shallows of emptiness, was the reasons why my husband betrayed me before GOD word, but then reality sat in and he did what he wanted to do, no person can send anyone into laying down with another, it's not the devil it was him.

At this time, I was so done with trying to find hope in our unity, I buried myself in building my brand, it was my sexually release on life, I used all my unhappiness and remade my happy. The more money I bring in the more my husband was happy.

Kept Harold up out my face, the us was gone, the day I found out he gave me a sexual transmitted disease from being careless and irresponsible with a nasty hoe bitch.

I lost all respect I had for Harold, after so many years of cheating, being every bitch it was, now you bring me a std, you didn't love me, how could you.

I had everything I wanted but Blacc, why he couldn't have been the man I was devoting this foundation to. It's been about four years since I saw him, and during this time me and my husband was really on some separation shit.

By this point Harold lived in a different state and I was just trying to find me, I had a house, a few cars, my kids were taken care of, money in the bank, my business was doing great, but I didn't have the man I wanted.

As always, I broke down and made that call to Monica, and she came thru like always. I invited Blacc to my house late one night, As I gave Blacc directions to my house, my heart was beating fast, my pussy was getting wetter, my mouth was watering.

Blacc pulled in my driveway, looking better than the last time I saw him, he been eating well I see, damn I was so happy to see him; my baby was sleep, so we didn't wake her.

Blacc knew I wanted him, as we talk about the positions, I like for him to do the most to and with me.

When he laid me down, all the memories of us played in my head, from Bellflower on back, our first time, and the last, his sex was on his grown man, the ate the pussy different, like he had years of practice, he caress my insides more meaningful, his kisses was more erotic and direct, why do I always fall for him, why wasn't he never my man.

Blacc conversation this time was more on what our plans should be, without directly saying I'm feeling you, let's try this out him mouth, I got scared, I was scared that he was lying, acting like he wanted to pursue me and us in a way I wasn't emotionally ready to explore with anyone, my husband took me thru the ringer so much all my trust in men was gone, I didn't want to become a sexual victim of Blacc or his dick.

His loving was an emotional rollercoaster, maybe I was reading more than what he was putting out there, he held me a little closer than the last time we were parallel to each other, I smiled myself to sleep, then it was time for him to leave, as the sun was breaking thru the twilight, I was watching him depart, I think I just needed to have him one more time.

I talk with Blacc as he drove all the way back to San Bernardino to ensure he made it home safe and sound, and the next day I declined to answer my phone. I didn't use him for sex; I need to see if I still had the persuasion to get him in my bed.

I could have easily invited him back over, for round two or more, but I decline to accept what he was offering, I was afraid that his commitment only consisted of his package when he was only in my presence.

Chapter 19

One last time again

Although my husband and I were separated, I still had hope that sometimes things would have been different, somehow. Seeing Blacc that night made me appreciate having a family with Harold. Blacc wasn't a bad dude, but his feeling for me was always questionable.

While Harold was away, he ended up getting sick, I felt obligated to have to go get him, and nurse him back to good health, he was still my husband, and the only father my kids known.

Harold of course soaks up every morsel of me, I knew I didn't want him no more, the thing was now when was he going to realized I didn't.

Time came and went and came and went, here it is almost three years, of me hating the pure sight of him, I was waiting on anyone or anything to take me far from here, a bull with rope dragging me thru an open fire would have been better than this mental torture of pretending marriage.

Things between Harold and me hit rock bottom, to the point where I was happy to be free of his hateful ways. I didn't date anyone, but I did have options if I chose to indulge. Harold was back out of state this time we both agreed with the change.

I finally found some peace. I had recently finished my first book and produced my own documentary, so I was pretty busy, but now that social media is at an peek of everyone fingertips, I decided to get and Facebook account, and find old classmates or friends I lost contact with over the years.

I found Blacc profile so we started mutual conversations about life and its ups and downs, he was a truck driver now, how he was married and unhappy, good for me, I thought, by now he had just amount the same children as I did, with different women. I could see that he was a man that likes to fuck.

We talked all while he was on that delivery in Arizona. Blacc appeared to have missed me also by his conversations, we both agreed that we would meet and hook up at a nearby hotel when he drops his last load off somewhere in Fontana, since I would be out his way anyways that night.

As plan we hooked up in a cozy standoff motel near the freeway entrance, the sex was alright, we haven't been with each other in years, my memory of us, had almost completely vanished, it was like trying something new, with someone new, really awkward and strange, his head was still bomb, maybe our disconnect might have been because he had been tired from driving, I don't know what it was. But I figured I will try it again to make sure.

He went back out of town and when he returned I gave him my home address, but he had to come past at night, I didn't want my neighbors to see a random dude coming to my house just in case my husband and I ever got back together.

I didn't have to worry about my children seeing him, they would be sleep. Only one of my kids I was worried about seeing him was my eldest, who burst in my room when I told him he was there, he hadn't saw him in years he missed him also.

As we were in my bedroom, Blacc asked if he could take a shower, I gave him a face towel and dry towel and lock my room behind me, I gave him enough time to prepare himself for me. I was nervous this time, my heart was beating fast. I took the slowest walk back up my stairs, politely knocked on my door, and when I closed the door behind me, I knew it was going to be good.

I was standing by my dresser facing the mirror, and Blacc came from behind me and lifted up my dress, his towel drop as I felt it hit my ankles, before I could say a word, Blacc had me bent all the way over touching the tips of my toes, serving my pussy, he knew how to get me ready. We were going at it like two crazed cats. His tongue massaging my inner thighs, making me moist, and his fingers inserted into my vagina, in and out.

Blacc picks me up in the air as I hold tight around his neck, he's pounding my guts loose, my body began to shake uncontrollably, he lays me back across my bed and open my legs as far as they could go and press firmly on my inner thighs to keep me from running as he ate me out.

I loved this shit, Blacc was down there for at least fifteen long minutes while I beg his to put it back inside me, once his dick enter my body I bust hot cum on his dick head, he loves this shit, we fuck like rabbits the remainder of the night I fell to sleep on top of him. Blacc dipped out before the sun rose, and I slept the entire day away.

When I got up, I didn't notice that Blacc had continually called my phone. When I did get in touch with him the conversation was much more inviting than any before, he was saying some good shit thru that telephone line, this time he was really on some let's see where this goes, and my heart was like hold the fuck up bitch, this aint what you want, he's married, regardless, if he say he's not happy, he was married, he needed to work that out with her first.

I couldn't continue this affair. I didn't need any more heartache, if he decided to return home, I know how that could be, I have been doing the same thing with my husband for years, and I was not going to be the side bitch or mistress.

Last time I talk to Blacc I found every reason why he should never call me again. I told him all sorts of mean, disrespectful things about his manhood, love making and personal self; I needed him to never entertain any thoughts of us ever. I knew he would never contact me again. As much as the things I was saying might have hurt him, they hunted me while I said them.

Chapter 20

I'm sprung there's no denying it

Not long after that, I found it in my heart to seek Blacc out again, but this time it was straight let's make some money together shit. One of his children mothers was in a bind and need some quick cash, I gave her the hook up for a small fee, long story short, both him and her tried to play me out some change.

Now this was an all-time low for Blacc, he on that grimy shit, damn I must have really hurt his feeling when I called him those names, funny part was, it was some change that they got over on, shit I spend within a twenty four hours period, me and him could have made more money than that, but he choose to burn his bridges for one of his bust ass baby mamas.

About a year later, I was in Wal-Mart in Foothill and I saw Blacc and his wife in the store, I didn't say anything or acknowledge them, but I did observed how distance they were while shopping, no physical connection at all, it was hilarious to see how unhappy happy people maneuver in public at least with Harold we pretended very well for the public viewing.

My oldest daughter had got herself in some trouble, so I had to move back to Los Angeles, and in doing so I moved right back to the same neighborhood I last saw my grandmother alive. I found out that the saying about life is a full circle don't always mean you revert to a child in your older days, my circle came, when I had to be faced with my fears of going back to where I ran from.

Having to be Westside Mamas again, thinking about my survival physically, the hood was a place you learn from not a place you indulged in. I had children now, the things I did when I was younger is not the same things these kids are doing now. My children knew nothing about that LA city life, they originated from Corona, the city that was ran by the KKK, and crime free living.

I knew that my time here was temporary I couldn't do this shit. I couldn't live this way, I made as much money as possible, and when I moved to Ohio I had twenty nine thousand, three hundred and seventy two dollars, minus the truck rental, gas for my truck, and my deposits on our new home in Cleveland.

It's funny how one simple thing can bring two people together, who would have guessed that both our passion for the open highway, speed, chrome, and mutual friends would have led me to a familiar Facebook account. I knew it was him, although he was much thicker, and had a full face on, I just knew, Naw, I knew it was him when I strolled thru his facebook's friends and saw someone with my name, oh he was looking for me too, I thought.

As I'm trolling his account, I see that his son passed away, an immediate shock to my heart, it's always sad when someone young passes away, no matter how death came. I needed to see if my friend was okay. I reached out with a: noticeable comment "looking good" on one of his photos, I'm sure if he saw the face, he would know who I was.

I sent him a friend request; if he wanted to link up, he would accept and respond.

Blacc click confirm and sent a message with his number. We would talk almost daily passing the time away with each other. Blacc was still a trucker and married unhappily so he said, I on the other end was again separated from my husband, who lived in Portland at the time, and me being a new a resident to this state.

Our common interest currently was our affiliation to the MC world, Blacc was a VP of a MC club, and I was a secretary of a social club. I didn't have an issue traveling or being social; therefore, me leaving on out of state runs was what I did often. I wonder how things would have played out if I saw him in Fresno or at Desert Soul, these two events be popping. I wasn't dating, trying to date, wanting to see, or needed any male companionship, I was cool loving myself. Were both married single?

We both decided to see each other face to face, so when he came back out here for a delivery we could meet. Instantly my heart skips, but not because I was sexually frustrated, but just seeing him after so many years was scary, we are really two different people that lived lives without each other, who was this stranger, I'm sure that ran across both our minds.

It's always good to be around him, our conversations were just as if we always stayed in contact, reminiscing about the days my grandmother was alive, that bucket car with no floor, bellflower, how he used to dip on me, and come back like everything was cool, by the ways our conversations were heading were in a direction of forgiveness on both of our behave. I was grown now, and I didn't have time to carry any more weight than I could bare, I had my own issues going on, we were good.

Every time he came out this way we would sit and talk, then one day we took it to the next level, I allowed him to lay me down again, what I do that for, I was lonely and missing that type of affection from the right opposite sex, he pulled me right back into the age of seventeen, I'm sprung, it's no denying it, I was hook.

I knew that he said he was governmental married, meaning his and her names were registered as each other's spouse, but his actions were that of a single man, once we lay down together, it was over, I no longer thought about the interruption I could have caused in his household. He was mine. This had to be destiny, how could we continue to meet each other in this lifetime, and not connect the right way.

Chapter 21

Motorcycle shit

I finally in a place in my life where I could see the us happening, but the both of us are in marriages it done matter how unhappy will tell each other we are with our partners we just couldn't just up and bounce, we both understand that commitments were formed, understanding were made and order must follow so no-one is just thrown in a pit of fire and dysfunction. We both had families.

I hit rock bottom, no because of something I did but because I allowed my oldest to interfere with my livelihood. Every parent's nightmare where your child is too smart to know they are making stupid ass mistakes, regarding the only person that always had they back. Apparently, her mistakes caused me to become homeless for the second time.

Blacc wanted me to find a place so me and kids didn't have to stay in a hotel, but I still had Harold, Blacc was not going to move me somewhere with my kids and have my nigga live in my house don't know any real man that would.

I felt that Harold should have stepped his game up instead of waiting on me to fix our living situation problem, but he took his sweet time. If any time before he needed to show me that he was for this family this would have been the perfect time. Here I was with a man I wanted to let go of, and the man I wanted.

I can deny that I cared for Harold for all the years we invested good and bad, at one point in this relationship I loved him to death, but my old love and new love was a train wreck, I still choose on him to decide our family sake even though it was when he felt like it.

Blacc was constantly in my ears about how I allowed myself to get in this situation how I wasn't person he knew, how I changed and just gave up, but his hounding towards me wasn't helping it was my reality that my life was fucked up, I'm sure that was Blacc's way of trying to get the old Stacy back on track, but it made me want to run, run away from every reminder of this undetermined displacement.

Blacc never didn't grasp that something was going on with me eternally that I couldn't foresee or prevent, he always talks about how I let go of my hustle. I was breaking down from the inside out. I been strong for too long, I been the fixer, the provider, the mother, the friend, the nurturer, the one who makes everyone feel better, the one who gives my last, and the lover but never been loved.

Although we now resided in a hotel, it didn't stop me from seeing Blacc he was my escape, of this hell hole of life in which I lived, besides the few new friends I met here in Arizona and on this motorcycles shit.

I could tell Black didn't too much care for me being on the set by the warning he use to give me about the MC world, the men and how not to become a set rat, but overall, I was already an active member of a club.

I know the main thing that Blacc told me was that if I ever fucked with a nigga on the MC set, he wouldn't ever mess with me again. But this was my happy.

I didn't do the standard set female stuff, but instead I am building a brand, a new alter ego, someone looked just met and not knew, I didn't change my personality of characteristics, and I just improved on my social skills.

Blacc would come down to Phoenix when he wasn't driving on motorcycles runs; I recall the first time Harold saw him on the set.

.

We were at Desert Dogg's MC annual picnic and Blacc was there. I made sure he saw his daughter. I gave them some private time, while I maneuvered within the crowd's doing my magazine stuff. Later that night was the big annual dance; I need a way to tell Harold that Blacc was in town without looking like I planned it.

I already knew he was here, but I needed a way to bring Harold into the situation without being sneaky and aware that Blacc even function on the set. We were at this annual and I walk outside to see if I saw Blacc or any of his club members, he told me they were coming; I was outside of the venue smoking a cigarette when I saw him.

Looking over my shoulder hoping Harold didn't come out to look for me. I waited till Blacc and his members were off their bikes and I went back inside.

When Blacc and his club walk in the door I walk out, hoping to brush against his body. Typically, on the set everyone hugs, a very friendly atmosphere, so we get Blacc and his members were out it wouldn't be strange to give out hugs, but I fucked up bad, when I hug Blacc.

I went straight in, titties on his chest pussycat touching his private area, that's not how normal bros and sisters hugs, my hug indicated a connection, either beginning or established, and my hug was more of a fifth teen second hug verse the hot four second one. I told on myself I said. I guess because the crowd was so huge nobody paid it any attention.

I told Harold I just saw Blacc and that he was in MC club, Harold low-key trip out on me, somewhat embarrassing, I tried my best to stop him for making a fool out the both of us, he was tripping big time.

I was so embarrassed, I hope Blacc wasn't looking at this fool put on this show, I did everything to stock Harold's ego, dance with him, dance on him, whisper things in his ear, he wasn't having none of that, anything to see him believe I was only there for him. It seems that Harold was following every move Blacc made that night, if Black went outside so did Harold, Blacc wasn't trying to check for me that night, I did too much trying to make sure Harold didn't trip out. I was really hoping Harold didn't do the super extras and Blacc come to where I was trying to intervene.

Me catering to Harold that night I believe I think I was trying to secure my knowing. The knowing that if this thing me and Blacc got don't work, I still have Harold. Blacc was pissed, trust he talked major shit, but in reality he wasn't just going to go home one day and tell his wife I'm leaving you to fuck with Stacy, he demand a lot of me but he was only giving me his words in return, so how do you choose familiar surroundings for unknown promises.

Chapter 22

Two at one time

A club in California was having a woman on the set appreciation dance on February 27th; it would be the perfect time for an out of state getaway with Blacc.

I made the hotel reservations, told him the date, and he made sure he was there. No-one knew that I was going to be leaving that night with him, I watch him all night like a middle school crush, when he hugged the opposite sex my heart would slightly give.

I hated that he was sharing him with others, I was never jealous of females until they're in his contact, always wonder if he slept with any, did he fuck them like he do me, did he suck the soul out when he was giving them head, I started to hate set bitches overall, because I never knew if he fuck one of them or not and his ass would lie and say he didn't just to appease me.

Black had a club member that was the only female in his club, and I always thought he lied on his dick when he said he never fucked. I found it hard to believe she was very attractive, dress real seductive damn near half naked, and had a rep for fucking a lot of men on and off the set, which was always in the mouths of the ugly monkey butt smelling bikers.

Black denied time and time again but in the eyes of the public they were fucking, the both of them moved in unity, she constantly hanging on his arms, especially in photos, she only draped on him, half naked, tittie's in his face every part was exposed but the nipples, and his solid hands on her waist fingertips planted on her half covered ass, but hay that's the same shit couple do.

Blacc flaunted his member like a mantel piece, it was hard to believe what he kept telling me, I'm sure it was more than what he was telling me, if everyone else around assumed then I wasn't tripping, I was seeing the same shit everyone else saw, two mother-fuckers that fuck and might still be.

Blacc will never tell me, I thought the old stick my dick in any and everything grew the fuck up, but again I guess not. I didn't care what plans they had tonight was mines.

I observed Black as he took down a few drinks that night, and in my head, I was thinking he going to dog fuck me. When he was ready to leave, he gave me the eye, I said my goodbyes, and we walk towards his black Tahoe, with all black matte rims. All I kept thinking was this nigga really do too much, but in a sexy way. I always liked that cocky confident arrogant way he had of showing off.

We got to the room he promised that he would be able to stay all night. I was hungry so he went and got me some food, when he came back I was waiting for him in a matching lace bra and panties set, after we ate, we fucked, and this wasn't the we in the truck fuck, but we passionately explored each other, his sex was always over the top mentally, we both cuddle and went to sleep about five I'm being woken by his hard dick sliding back in, it was a good hurt, my lips was swallowed but his dick was delicious.

It clamps to my walls, his stroke was softer but deep, he took his time and took care of me, by six-thirty in the morning he claims he had to take him son to football practice and will return before my check out.

Blacc left and didn't return, he made me feel cheap. He had to rush home to be family guy, see these are the things that wasn't consistent with him, and part of the reasons why I started to act different with him, she not going nowhere and no matter what he says he loves her and that's really where he wanted to be, was I the side-chic.

Late March I went to hospital because I had a cold that wouldn't break, from chills, sweats, fever, sore joints, mucus brown and yellow, this wasn't a regular cold, this was the second or third time I been to the hospital because I'm sick. I never in my life ever felt so ill.

I was so over these people telling me it's just an upper respiratory infection, I decided to go to another hospital for a second opinion. While I was there waiting on these labs and my test results to come in, a nurse comes in and tells me that my pregnancy test was positive, also my iron was extremely low, but the surprise of the day was me having walking pneumonia.

I could go home and given a lot of medication for the pneumonia, and a follow up appointment with an OBYGN. I was in so much pain and discomfort from the infection I totally forgot about the news of a baby, when I was feeling better I finally told black, he appeared not to be upset, he seemed okay with whatever decision I wanted to make, but he did stress the importance of my health with the baby.

I knew it wasn't no way Harold that it was his, I had stop having sex with Harold after he got tested positive for Hep C.

April passed then the beginning of June, and I was getting worse, I couldn't eat, drink, it was hard to breathe, I felt like I was going to die, by now I'm 18 weeks along, and I'm carrying twins, but my body was breaking down tremendous. Blacc again appeared to be with whatever I wanted as far as the babies was concerned but again, he was worried about my health.

One day I went to the restroom, and sat on the toilet, then I felt something weird in my lower abdomen, but I still didn't worry, but when I went to wipe the toilet paper was soaked with blood.

I open my legs and in the bottom of the reddish water was a blood clot the size of baby pacifier, blood was pouring out my vagina, the more I wipe the more it came.

My middle daughter walk in and saw all the blood, and quickly closed the door behind herself, she kept giving me towels to clean up with, I finally got out the stock of all the blood clots and bleeding and told her I needed to go to hospital.

Shortly after my arrival they confirmed I miscarried, but the strangest thing happens, I totally stop bleeding altogether. The next day u woke up feeling the best I ever had, about one week past and I got the chills out the blue, couldn't open my eyes, and was weak as fuck.

I needed medical attention fast, when I got to the hospital my body was had set up shock, apparently I had an incomplete miscarriage and the pneumonia was shutting down my systems, I was airlifted to another hospital for intensive treatment and emergency surgery, my blood pressure was 75/40 and dropping my blood count was at a 4, I was dying.

When I woke up I had already had surgery and was on non-stop antibodies, I was hospitalized for the next two weeks for treatments from the pneumonia, I recall the conversation that I had with Blacc when I was in recovery, how he wish he was there with me, and he felt sorry this happen, the first time in a long time he verbally express his concerns and they came from a place of sincerity and honesty.

I cried, and cried, I lost my sons on June 12, 2013. The weird part was that's the same month Shy was born.

Chapter 23

Been there, done that

I felt a loss of a different kind, a loss of wanting to hold or see someone, a loss of miss opportunity and obligations. I really wanted my kids, but it was God's will, I guess.

First time I ever experienced losing a child in that fashion, it was like having a force abortion, how would God interpret the death on judgment day would he claim it to be my fault or the fault of prescribed medication or it's prescribers.

Do I think Blacc was serious about wanting these children, frankly I don't know, I'm still unsure, but it did sound good. I need time for me I didn't want anyone in my immediate circle, my heart was hurting bad, why was God punishing me, u love being a mother and God was taking away the only thing in the world I was good at doing, maybe this was my eternal hell, the one people say we live in before death, my hell on earth.

Not being able to carry on a legacy of me, something I wanted all my life, little Me's to remind the world I existed somewhere, since I was always in hiding in the hearts of the men, I loved the most.

When I finally got my health back on track, I really was trying to experience life for what it was and had to give. Losing those babies brought on an urged of needing to complete my life quests and desires.

I needed to find my happiness for once, however it came. I was promised by God to receive if I believed in his words, and walk in his faith, as many times in my life I had to call upon his name for spiritual guidance and healing, God was going to make good of his promise to one of his faithful children. Reflecting all the times throughout my life I cried or was unhappy, my smiles awaited, I deserved it.

Harold knew that our relationship was at its end, especially when I became pregnant and the babies weren't his. I think he was happy that I lost the kids and ecstatic in the way I lost them; his hurt didn't compare to the hurt I will carry going forward.

Black and I continued to see each other, and his conversations were so misleading, he kept telling me to wait, he had things he needed to get right before he bounced on his wife, and I believed that he wanted me, I was waiting on him to correct his home life and we will soon build one of our own.

I had no intentions on being his side piece, I wanted the man, the man I wanted all my life, and I thought he wanted that also. One day when we were in his truck he got out, and his phone just happen to be sitting there, I contemplated overhand over if I should pick it up, and my head was saying no, but my heart was saying yes.

I read his messages with his wife, and realized all the things he was telling me was a lie, his conversations with her, didn't appear to be one of a man preparing to depart his wife, his was that of a man that was in love with his wife, her were the same, I felt betrayed, and angry, he's been living all this time, wanting me to get rid of my man for what he didn't have plans on leaving her, he wanted me for sex and friendship and her for his wife and companionship.

A harsh reality that this motherfucker been playing me now going on two years.

When he came back to his truck I was so furious, I just walk to my car, once I got in my car I text his lying ass and told him I read his messages, he tried to explain but, I didn't want to hear that shit. What could you possibly explain, how you used me, how you had no intentions of us, or how I misinterpreted everything you told me, and how you loved your wife, but lusted me?
I didn't want to hear none of that bullshit, I totally ruined any half ass relationships I had banking on your words of possibilities. Fuck his ass.

Well my stupid ass eventually fell back into Blacc's trap which leads me right to his bedroom. I found out I was expecting a little girl the later part of two thousand fourteen.

This time he wasn't happy, Blacc claims I was trying to set him up, like for real what could I get from him besides a hard dick and his lies of commitment to me when we were in each other presences besides those two he really had nothing to offer me.

I decided I needed to slow my availability to him down, make him think and decide if I was something he needed or wanted in his life. Blacc needs to weigh out his options because it was clear I wasn't one, but my pussy was a priority.

After my avoidance, Blacc began to become more persistent on seeing me, at first; my heart wasn't having his conniving ways. I was in my first trimester, and I really wanted my baby, not for him but for me.

Something about the whole experience was always satisfying to my soul. We went weeks at a time without physical contact, we would talk, but my soul didn't want to share any intimacy.

In late December of two thousand fourteen I was in a car accident, and I hit my stomach on the steering wheel which caused my baby to stop growing inside me. On top of all that stress I could name on one-hand how many times Black inquired about my baby.

When I had her he finally seemed a little concern, every blue moon he would voluntarily ask about her, I never trip I was used to raising his seeds by myself. My daughter was about two months old we started having sex again; I was back in the truck, seeing him least three times a week, Mondays, Wednesdays and Fridays.

I was over any possibility of us getting together, I was just content with the things as it was, nothing promised, and nothing committed. I like the fact that he wasn't my man, and didn't have to answer to me, it was a freedom partnership.

I didn't have to think twice if I found someone, I might have interest in, I had no obligations to Blacc he was still fucking both me and his wife.

I always felt if I was enough, he wouldn't need her, so therefore why not seek someone who could fulfill my void. I needed an relationship, it's easy to say you like being alone and single, but when you laying in your bed at night by yourself, no one-by-one hold you, rub your back, wake up too you get pretty lonely and easy mislead.

You start unconsciously seeking out special characteristics in an attractive personality and if you not smart enough you fall victim to an unwanted love, been there done that.

Chapter 24

Cancer

Black and I still manage to still share each other's company from time to time. One minute he's all into me, then by the end of the week he back being undecided, I just don't understand his thinking process.

Lately Black is always complaining that he's sick, something is always wrong with him, first he said he had a cold, then he said pneumonia, then he went to having severe back pains, his legs giving out, next constantly headaches.

I'm starting to believe that his wife is poisoning him, he never appears sick in my presence but soon as he gets home, he needs to go to the hospital for something, so he says, it's one or the two, and the two would be he's back lying again.

I got a strange friend request from his baby mama Toy, at first, I didn't know who it was, but the way my popularity was set up, I let a lot of unknowns watch my Facebook activity, they were my personal fans.

One particular day she comment on my Facebook post, so that made me troll her profile and I saw children that look like mines but didn't trip, you know the saying that all black people are related but those kids had his last name, and that's when I put two and two together, this bitch watching my page.

I use to wonder how Blacc knew things I was doing, I block his ass about four months ago for snooping on my page asking me questions and shit he had no business asking me about, he wasn't just my man, he was shared community property, so that meant he didn't earn the rights to question my whereabouts let alone my comings and goings anymore.

Blacc went from coming out here every other day to maybe once a month, I figure with all his lying he's been doing lately about being sick and shit he was up to his games of dick and other people's pussy, or he was trying to repair his household.

January 2015, Blacc and I got into an awful argument behind his baby mama. Toy and I got into a Facebook argument and the slick bitch started saying things only he would know, so in return I said things I shouldn't have known, back and forward and guess who runs to this bitch rescue, yes Blacc like he always have.

I'm always wrong even when she starts the shit; it's baffling how he always wanted me to act like an adult dealing with this childish bitch. Nevertheless, me and Blacc are now not talking again behind this bitch, this is the second time he played me for this hoe, and the third time he played me for a bitch who have sucked his dick.

I was so angry at him and her, I didn't even get the chance to tell him I was again pregnant, nor the opportunity to tell him I lost the baby fighting for him to see I was in the right this time and his baby mama was the shit starter, that called his wife and told her about me and my children with him.

Because if I would have done something like that I would have told her our history, and how much I lust and loved the man she pretends to love, how he only married her because I was selfish and constantly denied any solid commitment I could have formed with Blacc, he will always be a part of me, and no matter how our lives develop I will always be a part of his, and she will always be a "After-me"

I might not surface for years on years, but whenever he needed or wanted me, I will always be there, the paperwork they both signed made her his, but my heart made him mines.

One day in late February, I was lurking on Facebook and I see his sister Monica put up a post about praying for her little brother as he's battling cancer and posted a picture of Blacc. I immediately felt a broken heart. It's like my throat was block, and I couldn't swallow.

My mind left my body and I was unable to think, my heart stop and my airways collapse, my eyes filled with water and my vision became blurred, my hand tremble and my legs buckled. I know he had said something about being tested for, but I just thought he's lying again, he's too healthy to be sick.

I text his phone, with a screenshot of her post, is this true? I couldn't wait for a reply I called his phone, his voice sound weak, and painful, his voice was hoarse and forced, "*Is this true?*", I asked, he got quiet, I could tell that he didn't want to tell me, his heart was hurt, I just hung on the phone inhaling his breathing sounds, he finally said the words that pierce my heart with soaked darts of what am I going to do. *"Yes...."*

When you Think of Cancer, you immediately think of the worse. Right now, my head's filling with everything unreal. visions of me waking up to find out I missed another opportunity of happiness, to have not been able to give my all to this one man and have my heart solely alone after I dedicated over twenty plus years to this one person, imaginings the us with hopes that one day he will finally be mines and were both in a commitment that's established.

What about my children, they children, his family, and family members?

What was I to do, and the list continued, which made me panic and have anxiety attacks, that was the selfish me? Although he's in a battle for the remainder of his life, his outcome affects me, we're in this together.

Thinking about all the times I thought he was lying and trying to avoid me, oh how I wish I was there to closely watch him, frantically embrace his emotions, surpass his hurt, and completely act like cancer was a cold that will be gone soon. Wishful thinking.

To realize this man can't be defeated in any of his life's trials or tribulations. As I have known for him to be a fighter and an act type of dude. Victoriously Remarkable. I finally saw him face to face and I looking at a stranger, he lost so much weight; his body is altering with apparatus to help fight this demon. I was scared to touch his body, for him to touch mines, I didn't want to hurt him or cause any discomfort, he kept saying it's okay, but I'm looking in his eyes and it's not. Blacc held me a little closer spoke a little longer, his hug was a little tighter, laughed a little louder, and he smiled all night long. Impressive.

I didn't want to leave his side. When I shared my hearts hurt my ones closest to me, I had friends reach out to me that was familiar with our history with their shared their concerns, some prayers, well wishes that everything will be okay.

Others express sincere hopes, and recommendations, and I thought over and over in my brain, I was on an emotional rollercoaster and was travelling in a complete mental breakdown time warp.

The next time I was with him my life was waken with the idea of things will be back to normal soon, I became mentally ready, ready to stand right beside my man in this journey, ready to defend this intruder that wants what I work so hard to get, vesting.

Hearing him say he's dying ate at my soul, like hungry ghetto wire rats crossing paths with cat that haven't eaten in weeks, who is now on a mission of survival. I need him to keep me strong, keep what part of me only I shared with him safe.

Blacc said *"He don't need folks acting different with him, he's still the same person he was before he got sick"*. Prideful.

I can go on and on expressing how my how much I adored him, but to sum up all the miscellaneous adjectives, nouns, verbs, etc., I'm going leave you with one word, blessed!

Every time I left his presence, I would sit in my car for at least an hour before going back home, and I would bellowed uncontrollably, asking God to made sure Blacc spirits never once decrease, comforted my children, to always make all his tomorrows as normal as possible giving his circumstances, and to prepare me for whatever God had plan.

Each time I saw him afterwards, I always tried to make it the best, always shared laughs and reflected on our friendship history, I tried my hardest to never break down in his presence, but at times while he held me tears of sadness will escape, the possibilities of one day this union will end, and I'm left behind to wish to one day we see each other again in our afterlife.

Chapter 25

My well is dry

I got over the days of "What if's" and turned them into "Every chance I get". These pass nine to ten months have been great, Blacc goes to chemotherapy and rest at home a few days, and when he hits the road he always headed in my direction.

His body is amazing, he got really chiseled and the weight lost looks kind of sexy, he eats a lot healthier and his spirits are more pleasant.

Blacc love making at times can be complicated not because he can't get up or perform, but it appears to be more draining than fulfilling especially right after any chemo treatment.

Blacc always has a way of asking that question, *"What am I going to do when he passes?"* I wish he stop trying to prepare me, I accepted the fact that the possibilities might happen, but my faith in my constant talks with God on his behalf reassures me everything will soon be fine.

One day he won't have to worry about the cancer in his body, he will wake up healed, blessed with years of living and me under his arm.

Blacc has asked me a few times to go out of town with him, and sometimes I get scared thinking he might pass while we together and I will flip the fuck out. I have those kinds of dreams often especially when he asks me my plans if something should happen.

Sometimes I wish Blacc would man up and tell his wife about me, not the freak part, but let her know about our friendship so if anything was to ever happen to him, I would have to find out on Facebook. I have no issues with her. I look at it like this if their union was so scared then I wouldn't be their third wheel.

We're both in love with him for our own personal reasons. She has hers and I have mines and at the end of the day he in the start of our common interest.

If I ever need to come take care of him I would, I would sit by his side, and read corny love stories out loud, yell out freaky sexual things to do while I grab his balls, tell unfunny jokes, say things of sarcasm, and repeat whatever endlessly, things I know that would make him smile, that's my friend, we been friends for too many years, that's my children father, my first love, the man that owned my heart, and didn't know how to make it his, the first man I ever explored sexuality with mentally, the man I could never delete, My man.

Who would have figured that road trip we took of June two thousand seventeen was the last time I was able to see my friends face? I have memories, I watch him while he drove, sometimes pretending to be sleep, I memorized his movements, all our years of us replayed over and over, I cried slightly.

One night I recall rubbing his back and tears filled up in my eyes would this be the last time, how many more times do I have left? I made sure we talk about things in our past that we didn't correct then, he asks questions, and I did too, I think our us had an understanding, we will always be friending no matter what or how.

As I stand before you, looking into your casket, I'm happy you finally found peace, you don't have to suffer anymore, I always thought when this day happen, I would lose my mind, but you prepared me.

I promise not to cry today as my heart is filled with us, I can't say that every day I won't miss you and become isolated and distance, but I will try my hardest to smile, because you were special to me, you were my friend, my family and my man.

Rest in Peace Blacc, my well is finally dry.

This book is dedicated to a special person in my life that gave me my motivation back Marvis, For a year you allowed me to sit down and regain myself back, not all days were good, but you stayed on my butt hard, and your words and wisdom gave me strength like no other. I'm forever grateful for your friendship.

I recall you always telling me to be great at something I'm good at, and writing was my gift. I want you to know that I valued yourself worth like no other, you will always be special to me, and carry a piece of my heart where ever I go in life, you gave me back my gift to be great again, you took the time out to invest mentally in me, when I forgot who I was, and gave me lessons about life I will never forget. What didn't kill me, made me stronger.

Forever Your Friend, Celestinia